HOW TO DESIGN & BUILD
CHILDREN'S PLAY EQUIPMENT

*Created and designed by
the editorial staff of
ORTHO BOOKS*

Editor
Barbara Ferguson

Assistant Editor
Teri Lammers

Projects Designer
Jay Beckwith

Writers
Jay Beckwith
Craig Bergquist
Ron Hildebrand

Illustrators
Craig Bergquist
Ron Hildebrand
Mark Pechenik

Major Photographer
Steve Marley

Ortho Books

Publisher
Robert L. Iacopi

Production Director
Ernie S. Tasaki

Managing Editors
Michael D. Smith
Sally W. Smith

System Manager
Leonard D. Grotta

National Sales Manager
Charles H. Aydelotte

Marketing Specialist
Susan B. Boyle

Operations Coordinator
Georgiann Wright

Office Assistant
Marie Ongsiaco

Senior Technical Analyst
J. A. Crozier, Jr.

Chevron Chemical Company
6001 Bollinger Canyon Road, San Ramon, CA 94583

Acknowledgments

Composition and Pagination
Linda M. Bouchard

Copy Chief
Melinda Levine

Copyeditor
Judith Dunham

Indexer
Frances Bowles

Photo Editor
Cindy Putnam

Production Artists
Deborah Cowder
Lezlly Freier
Anne Pederson

Proofreader
Leslie Tilley

Project Builder
Curt Wear, Novato, Calif.

Additional Photographers
Heidi Bishop: pages 9, 10, 16, 17
Alan Copeland: pages 6, 14
Jim Dennis: front cover, pages 3 (top),
 4–5, 12
Raymond Quinton: pages 7, 11, 36

Photo Stylist
JoAnn Masaoka

Consultants
Robert J. Beckstrom, Berkeley, Calif.
Anthony Rudl, Glen Gardner, N.J.

Special Thanks to
Cecily Beckwith, Hannah Beckwith, Jordan Burns, Skylar Bishop, Chuck Cilley, Danny Garretson, Allison James, Elizabeth and Michael Keiser, Brianne Kennedy, Christopher and Matthew Long, Spencer Marley, Alyssa Matheson, Kevin O'Sullivan, Rachel Palacios, Miles Pederson, Cory and Loren Pullen, Heidi and Shantelle Salyer, Larry Sherman, Julie and Mark Van Velzen, Whitney Tiedemann, Graham and Lacey Waldon, Danielle and Jason Wessel

Lithographed in U.S.A. by
Webcrafters, Inc.

Front cover. The Creative Climber is a multilevel structure with options for slide, fire pole, and swings. The design and building instructions begin on page 64.

Title page. Pull-up bars, parallel bars, swings, horizontal ladder, seesaw, slide, and fire pole all combine to make the Fitness Gym provide both fun and loads of exercise. See page 53.

Back cover:
Upper left. A-frame Clubhouse, pg. 41
Upper right. Fitness Gym, pg. 53
Lower left. Creative Climber, pg. 64
Lower right. Split-level Playhouse, pg. 81

HOW TO DESIGN & BUILD
CHILDREN'S PLAY EQUIPMENT

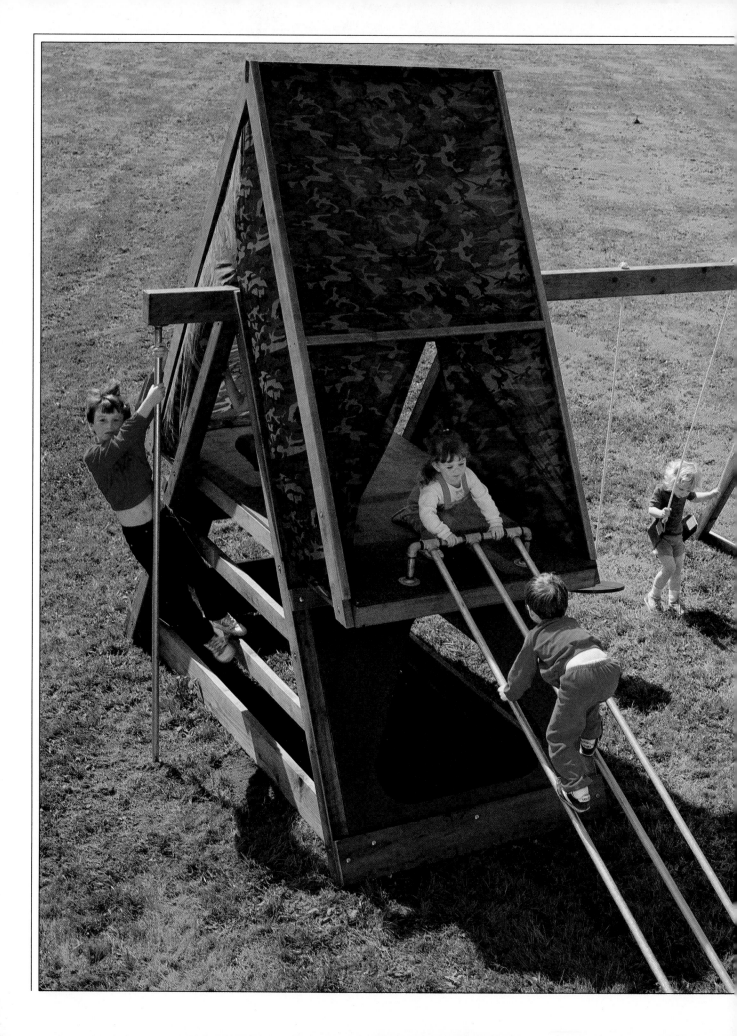

ELEMENTS OF PLAY

Many conventional play equipment systems are available in stores. Most likely, you selected this book because you want to provide your child with a special place to play in your backyard. The projects described in this book are creative alternatives to standard playground equipment—alternatives that both you and your child should find more satisfying.

The best play happens when a child has many things to do, big and small, active and quiet. The play structures in this book not only provide this type of varied environment, but function as frameworks for growth and learning. Here in Chapter 1, you will find small projects such as swings, slides, and sandboxes. These can be used alone or in conjunction with the four large projects described in Chapter 2. The large projects can be built in phases, if you choose, so that they grow with your child.

To select the right structure and to understand which parts will be used at various ages, some basic facts about stages of growth and learning are helpful. The following pages provide a brief summary of child development through play.

The A-frame Clubhouse, page 41, appeals to a wide range of ages because its design allows a variety of activities. A child can swing and climb with friends, or use it for a quiet place to read or play alone.

Play and learning

Play is a great teacher throughout childhood. Unlike simpler species, humans continue to play throughout their lives. Being a skilled player is valued because it implies a high degree of mastery. In history, education and play have been viewed separately, but in recent years there has been a growing awareness that play helps to develop skills in conceptual thinking. With this understanding comes a concern for the quality of play for modern children who may be entering a "school" setting at two years of age or younger.

Physical skills learned during play are basic to success in the classroom. Every first-grade teacher can tell you stories about children who have difficulty developing writing skills because when they move one hand the other hand moves as well. Being able to move individual parts of the body while the rest of the body remains still is part of many childhood games.

The ability to read a line of text is fundamentally a physical skill. Some children have problems reading because their poor eye coordination prevents them from maintaining their place on the page. Eye doctors have noticed a disturbing trend in modern children. Many children see well enough when looking straight ahead but have poor peripheral vision. Too much television watching is suspected to be the cause. Visual perception is significantly improved through play. A game of tag, for example, requires good peripheral vision.

Being able to focus on objects both near and far also requires motor development. In this case, the eye muscles are receiving the workout. A good place for this exercise is on a swing because motion requires constant changes in focus. Once this is learned, children can catch a moving ball as it nears them.

From the millions of objects in the environment, how do children discover what is important to look at, to hear, and to smell? Many children

Many different physical skills are involved in executing a successful cartwheel (above) or hitting a moving ball with a bat (left). Not the least of these is the ability to focus one's eyes correctly in order to balance or take aim. This can translate into the ability to follow a line of text while reading.

have difficulty discerning figure from background. Some do not read by looking at the letters; rather, they see the surrounding space. For them *wear* is the same as *were*. By exploring the environment through play, such children learn through direct experience what is object and what is background.

Children must have a mental image of their body in order to move through space. This is not as simple as it sounds because a child's body is rapidly changing in both size and proportion. Not only is body image key to movement, but it underlies such important perceptual abilities as directionality, judging relative sizes, and defining relationships of objects in space. Length, height, area, and volume are just a few of the concepts a child learns while moving in play.

Movement such as running, throwing, and swimming are actually composed of many smaller movement skills that must be strung together in a series. Fundamental to most logical and intellectual thinking, the ability to make these chains is first learned in play. During play, movement chains are practiced repeatedly, until they become habitual patterns that free the intellectual parts of the brain for more learning.

These are but a few of the hundreds of ways that children's thinking is developed through play. But play is far more than just a tool by which children discover and organize their world. Play is also critical to the development of expressive capabilities. As those who work with disabled children are vividly aware, children who learn to play successfully with other children are on the road to leading normal lives. Through play, children learn to interact with others. When they invent pretend games and give each other roles, they are developing both communication and leadership skills. Being able to live within the rules of society is a complex challenge that is critically important to a child's success in life. Play provides the stage for practicing social skills.

Childhood's ages and stages

Educators have taken a long time to recognize that children have many different styles and rates of learning. Therefore, any list of stages will only approximate your child's actual ability. Children can be inconsistent: astounding us one day with their precociousness and regressing to infantile behavior the next.

Developmental guidelines can help you understand your child's uniqueness and can also help expose variations of talent. Parents should not, however, attempt to train specific skills in very young children but should focus on the total child. Building self-confidence in a two-year-old is much more important than teaching the child to catch a ball.

The first year
The parent is a child's first playground—jungle gym, swing, and merry-go-round. Numerous studies have established that physical interaction between parent and child is the essential first step in a child's growth. In one case, infants gently spun around each day on a swivel chair, in an adult's lap, showed significantly better movement skills than others who were not spun.

At this stage, the backyard is a place for an outing, and to experience it a child must be carefully supervised.

The second year
At two years, a child begins to move, and at this stage, safety is a primary need. The environment must have well-defined boundaries that not only exclude outside forces but also keep a child inside the play area. Most people are aware of the need for childproofing a house to remove dangers from the reach of young children. The same process must also be applied to the backyard.

A two-year-old is a great climber: at least great at going up, not always at getting down. Thus, climbing frames, while popular and necessary, should be used with supervision.

Filling and dumping, catching and letting go, and piling up and knocking down are some common play activities. A child at this age likes to play with sand, using buckets, blocks, and other loose objects. This experience needs to be introduced gradually since a child tends to experiment by enacting such thoughts as "I wonder what sand tastes like."

Primitive forms of dramatic play occur at the end of the second year, when an infant reproduces some of mother's actions. Animals become important, and stuffed toys are given play voices. The later stages of the second year can be a trial for parents. The only word that the child can say seems to be an emphatic "No!" At this age, children are often demanding and impatient, and may exhibit violent emotions. The play environment can be used to redirect these energies, instead of parents' having to confine a child with ultimatums.

The third year
Three-year-olds don't pretend to be Superman; they actually become the role. Roles constantly shift in this stage of dramatic play. One moment a child is playing house, the next firefighter. This is the time to provide props such as capes and hats. But be prepared to pick up after the games, since three-year-olds are not very good at cleaning up.

This is, however, an excellent time to teach good habits, because a three-year-old has become more cooperative.

At this age, a child begins to spend significant periods of time in unsupervised play. Generally, this play includes only one playmate since the social skills for group play are undeveloped. Items for construction, as well as props for dramatic play, are used at this age.

A three-year-old begins to master most of the fundamental movement skills and spends time practicing various tasks on play equipment. Activities such as going in and out, or being on top of or under, help a child learn orientation in space.

Right: Three-year-olds delight in acting out dramatic roles using props and simple costumes.

Below: In the second year, a child often plays in a make-believe world, needing only a special place and a favorite companion.

The fourth year

Four-year-olds are beginning to gain a sense of themselves as individuals. Dramatic play isn't restricted to playing house but is broadened to include the community at large. Playing astronaut, doctor, or storekeeper is acted out in detail. Masculine and feminine traits are exaggerated, and costumes must be complete in every detail. A simple hat no longer suffices to evoke the cowboy or cowgirl; belts, guns, gloves, and boots are needed as well.

This is the year of the clubhouse. Children enact attacks and rescues, and create "safe" places where "good guys" can escape from "bad guys." Monsters and wild animals are also part of complex games of chase.

Physical activity is at an all-time high, and every part of the play structure gets a workout. Cooperation between three or four children occurs with increasing frequency, as does constructive play. Movable parts on play structures, such as planks and fabric panels, are particularly useful.

The fifth year

At this age, there is continuity to a child's play, and a particular activity may be repeated and elaborated over several weeks. Play becomes a tool for modeling the world, and a child uses play to adjust to the demands of life.

Dramatic play now has complex dialogues and scripts. Puppet shows and romantic dramas are common. Constructive play, too, becomes realistic—as in making paper money to buy a pizza at a pizza factory.

For many children, hand-eye coordination has developed enough so that they can learn basic ball games. Some children may show interest in games with rules. Movement skills include skipping, hopping, galloping, and bouncing a ball.

"I can do it myself" is the motto of this age. Even when the task is beyond their skills, five-year-olds keep trying, often ending in tears of frustration. Because this is a time of testing, parents should watch their children's activities without volunteering help—which, in any case, would automatically be rejected.

The years six through eight

These are the years of skill development. At an earlier age, a child's body is basically a single unit. Now he or she is able to perform coordinated actions, for example, using a hammer with one hand instead of two. Skills performed singly by a five-year-old are combined and done simultaneously by a six-year-old.

Four-year-olds play in groups and begin to play simple organized games with rules.

10

Because of their high degree of movement skill, children at this age are interested in games with clear challenges and rules. Dexterity and balance have developed to the point that a child can stand on one foot with eyes closed.

The backyard play space becomes a child's personal territory, and elaborate changes are made. These modifications can include a variety of activities from painting to digging caves to carpentry. Parents should make an occasional safety inspection of the play area when it is unoccupied.

At this age, dramatic play normally takes on sinister overtones. Vampires and werewolves abound. Even benign characters can turn nasty in a flash. The family, and especially parents, are conspicuously absent from these dramas. Rather, the peer group becomes central, and generally boys and girls play in separate groups.

Eight years and beyond

The child now moves into the domain of sports and competition. It's not enough just to be able to do a pull-up; the preadolescent wants to know the statistics from the *Guinness Book of World Records*. Now is the time for parents to return to the backyard and begin to work out with their children.

If you haven't already, this is also the time to add fitness components to the play structure. For the next few years, until the onset of teenage separation, your relationship with your child can be close and sharing.

The backyard becomes a refuge from the real world. It will be a hangout both when the child needs to be alone and when "the gang" wants to get together. This is a good time to encourage your child to keep a diary and take pictures, which years later, will become personal treasures.

At this age, play can be transformed into a lifelong interest in physical fitness and participation in sports. The closeness you have with your children and their friends can form a basis of trust on which to build some of the solutions to the problems of becoming an adult.

As a child approaches 8 years, dexterity and coordination develop to a point where complex movement skills become possible.

Creating places to play

Now that you understand the importance of play in development and have a basic overview of the stages of childhood, you are ready to create spaces that foster play. Although the primary goal may be to build a backyard play structure, an understanding of fundamental design principles for play spaces will allow you to create play environments wherever you and your child may be—indoors, traveling in a car, or eating at a restaurant. Once understood, these principles are tools through which you and your child can adapt successfully to any situation.

Age appropriate

While the previous section is fresh in your mind, try to visualize your child in the spectrum of development. Remember a past incident between you and your child that was unpleasant. Chances are good that the conflict was due, at least in part, to expectations for your child's behavior that were beyond his or her developmental level. Look at the child's toy collection. Some toys are used frequently, others ignored. One of the main reasons for selective use of a toy is its match with a child's stage of growth.

If you monitor your child's use of toys, you can ascertain his or her developmental level. This knowledge assists in making decisions about what to include in a play environment, or what to expect in your child's behavior.

Complexity

The primary function of childhood is learning. Children focus most of their attention on discovering all they can about the world around them. Some people say that children have short attention spans; this just is not the case. In the right environment, children will play for hours at a time. What makes children appear to have short attention spans is the speed with which they learn all there is to know about a particular situation.

A parent's nightmare is waiting in an airport for a plane that is two hours late. For the first fifteen minutes, children will be interested in the planes coming and going. If you have a few treats in your pocket, children will last perhaps another five minutes. Getting to know the neighbors may take ten minutes. General running around, another ten. Now the situation starts to get difficult as children begin to explore ashtrays and bathrooms, and become restless. What happened? Having learned all they can from the environment, children seek more to discover. Wise parents know that an hour is about as long as they can reasonably ask children to wait. The problem can be solved by moving the children into a new space where there is more to explore.

Many parents understand this phenomenon, at least intuitively. Yet those same parents expect children to spend hours each day in a backyard that has less interest than an airport waiting area. A successful play space is one that contains sufficient objects to create a miniature world. The natural environment is complex; something new can be found under every rock. The goal of a play area should be to come as close as possible to reproducing the richness of nature.

If the environment is interesting and full of new things to learn, children will play quietly for hours.

Most play equipment is more interesting when shared with a friend.

Freedom of play

It does little good to have a rich and diverse environment if a child is not free to explore it. Consider the sandbox. This is a relatively simple environment, and yet it can involve the child for hours. The sandbox is most successful when it combines sand with water and a few sand toys. A child's freedom to move, shape, and control the elements of the sandbox will sustain his or her interest. Loose parts, such as the deck planks in the Creative Climber on pages 64–79, allow children to create new combinations and relationships among the elements.

Social interaction

This is the aspect of play that tends to be overlooked. When we ask our children to go outside and play, we envision the child playing alone. Children often play by themselves, but they are not alone. Even in solitary play, a child is embedded in the fabric of the family. Just as parents, returning from work, take time to share the activities of the day, so a child needs to feel his or her activities are part of the life of the family. Becoming involved with a child's daily activity is a good way to motivate creative play.

The other side of social play is providing for playmates. The designs in this book are intended to work best when used by two or more children. An important task for a parent is to arrange for the participation of other children.

When you create a rich and complex environment that is geared to your child's age and incorporates objects a child can move and change, you are well on your way to forming a successful play space. Adding playmates and making the play experience an important part of family life complete the process.

Safe fun

No place or activity can be completely safe. Indeed, protecting children in a padded cell would inhibit their learning. What you want is a place where children have the opportunity to fail—an environment where they can stretch beyond their limits under the watchful eye of a parent, fall, and get up to try again.

Safe play is challenging but not hazardous. A challenge is something a child can see and choose, whereas a hazard is an element or factor not apparent to the child. A good play environment has many challenges and no hazards.

The Consumer Products Safety Commission has information on playground safety. To obtain copies call the CPSC hotline (800) 638-2772.

The greatest hazard of play equipment is falling. The CPSC found that nearly 75 percent of the injuries related to play equipment resulted from falls. Two factors determine the extent of injury from a fall: height and impact surface. To protect children, a play structure should be as low as possible and still be functional. The designs provided in this book place children no more than five feet above the ground. The Creative Climber and Fitness Gym allow adjustment of the deck height as children mature.

The CPSC recommends that all playground equipment be installed over appropriate ground cover such as sand, pea gravel, small wood chips (¾-inch or smaller), or shredded wood chips. It should extend six feet beyond the structure in all directions. Since children usually jump out of swings, extra space should be provided in front and back of the swings.

When concrete is used for footings, the upper edges must be well below the sand. The surface of the concrete should be smooth and the edges rounded, just in case the footing becomes exposed in the future.

Other safety features should be considered. Small children sometimes put their heads into openings and then are unable to get out. To prevent this, openings must be larger than seven inches or smaller than four inches in diameter. Also eliminate V-shaped openings. Finally, do not let children abuse play equipment as this can make it unsafe.

Inspect play structures for protrusions. The most common are caused by bolts used to make connections. To avoid these, this book specifies recessed counterbores for all but the largest bolts. This detail requires additional time and equipment but reduces protrusion hazards. Where counterbores are not used, any bolt threads extending beyond the nut should be removed and filed smooth.

Sharp edges can also present hazards. When wood is used for construction, corners are easy to round. Lumber should be selected for its smooth surfaces free of splinters. One area to inspect with particular care is the bottom edge of the slide. Construction details specify that the slides are slightly wider than the sheet metal used for the bed so that the sharp steel edge is recessed.

The best way to teach children safety on play equipment is by example. Also, a very young or timid child will feel more secure if the first trip down a slide is in an adult's lap.

Teaching children about safety

Teach children safety rules with sensitivity, since they will find other places to play if the backyard becomes a place of *don'ts* instead of *do's*.

Here are some basic rules.

1) Do not throw sand or ground cover material.

2) Do not climb on the very top of the structure.

3) Do not tie ropes around yourself or others.

4) Put loose parts away when playtime is finished.

5) Do not climb with sticks in your mouth.

6) Wear nonskid shoes.

7) Never wear ponchos with hoods while playing on the structure.

8) Do not climb on the structure when it is icy and slippery.

9) Do not use equipment unless a parent is at home.

Preventive maintenance

Well-constructed play equipment requires little maintenance, but periodic inspections help prevent possible injury and protect equipment.

Ground contact. Look for exposed, cracked, or broken footings. Dig as deeply as possible below the sand and inspect wooden members for rot and termites. Replace defective parts with pressure-treated lumber.

Structure. Check for loose or broken members. Tighten bolts. Look for splinters or serious checking in wood, especially on the slide rails. Apply paint or sealer as required.

Play attachments. Check for structural integrity and secure anchoring. This may best be done by applying your own weight to the equipment. Give extra care to inspection of the attachment points for swings.

Ground cover. Be sure that at least six inches of material are present and that drainage is working adequately. Rake cover to a uniform depth.

Swings should be inspected periodically for wear on ropes and connections. Replace worn equipment promptly.

Hide-outs

When you begin to plan a backyard play space, you may think first of active play on swings and slides. But children actually spend more time playing pretend games. This imaginative play happens almost anywhere—in the back seat of a car, in the closet, up in a tree—but it flourishes wherever there is a sense of enclosure.

The ideal hide-out is not fully enclosed, however; it allows a child to see out without being fully visible. Hide-outs should be small and intimate. Those that are up in a tree or down in a hole have a special feeling. They are different from everyday life and therefore more exciting.

Tents

An easy hide-out to make is a simple pup tent constructed from a sheet of fabric or plastic, a rope connected horizontally between two supports, and four stakes or weights at the corners. Such a simple tent is still quite serviceable, despite its lack of sophistication, since it is used primarily during good weather.

Rip-stop nylon is an excellent material for tents. It is light, colorful, and durable. Hemming the edges of the rip-stop, although not required, is a good idea. A quick way to make sturdy rope connections is with an inexpensive grommet set.

Playhouses

A traditional playhouse consists of a little box with a peaked roof, a door, and one or two windows. Although the traditional playhouse is adequate just as it is, additions can enhance children's use for play. Playhouses are more interesting if they have curtains, secret passages, lookout windows or periscopes, and "treasure chests" for storage. The plans for the Split-level Playhouse on pages 81–93 show a design to which these features can easily be added.

For ambitious and skilled carpenters, Ortho's *Outdoor Storage* provides detailed instructions for the construction of an outdoor shed with

The tree house is a favorite type of hide-out for children. In a world where just about everyone else is taller, children occasionally enjoy standing above it all.

several variations. Following these plans, you can build a permanent structure that will serve handsomely as a playhouse while your children are young and later can be easily converted for storage.

Tree houses

Having a tree house is every child's dream: being up high in the wind, clouds, and leaves; spying out on people; and having a secret place. Since every tree is unique, plans for tree houses are infeasible. There are, however, a few rules to follow.

Trees are alive; they grow and move. A tree house must be designed to adjust to these changes. If the tree house will be removed in five years or less, simple nail connections to the tree will probably be sufficient. For a more durable structure, use large lag screws. Sometimes cable or wire is employed to lash constructions to trees. Although strong, this connection risks strangling the tree or limb as it grows.

The first and most important step in constructing a tree house is to determine a horizontal plane in the tree where a platform or floor can be built. Then build the rest of the structure from this base.

Access to tree houses is often made of boards nailed to the tree trunk. A safer solution is to construct a ladder. This is better for the tree, too. The ladder could be made from 2 by 4s with 1 by 4 rungs. A rope ladder is also easy to make, and children like them because they can draw them up to keep out the "bad guys." Assemble the ladder from wooden closet pole dowel and ½-inch polypropylene rope. Cut rungs to 18 inches, and drill two parallel ⅝-inch holes one inch in from each end. Thread rope through holes, and place a knot every 16 inches. To make climbing easier, provide a means of attaching the lowest rung to the ground to hold the ladder stable as children climb.

Grow a hide-out

Sometimes a simple solution will work as well as a complex one. You may have the materials for a hide-out right in your backyard. If you have a sturdy shrub or tree at least five feet tall, cut out the interior branches and leave intact as much of the exterior canopy as possible. Inspect the plant for strength so that you can alert your children to the safe places to climb.

If you lack a suitable tree and prefer that children avoid playing in the garden, you can grow a flowering or fruiting hide-out. All you need is a plot of soil, a trellis, and some seeds.

The trellis frame can be any shape, but arches and tripods are the easiest to build. Use lightweight wood or plastic pipe for the frame. Baling wire is a convenient material for lashing the structure together. It can also provide runners to support the vines, which will fill in the open areas.

Choose a hardy vine that spreads rapidly. Children especially enjoy plants that produce flowers or fruit. Mix perennials with annuals for the first couple of years until the slower growing vines are established. Prepare a rich, well-drained soil to promote rapid growth. When siting the flower bower, choose a location that provides several hours of morning or afternoon light rather than full sun so that the hide-out does not become too hot for the children. The following are recommended vines for growing your own hide-out.

Annuals: Scarlet runner beans, hybrid morning glory, potatoes, gourds, cucumbers, melons

Perennials: Clematis, trumpet vine, grapes, wisteria, honeysuckle, star jasmine, Virginia creeper

Children often find a canopy of shrubs with a hollow center to hide under. You can prune out inside branches to enlarge the play space.

SWINGS

Children like to swing and spin. Not only are these movements fun, but they help develop perception, balance, and agility. Pumping a swing requires considerable coordination and rhythm.

Because everyone remembers how much they enjoyed swinging, swings are usually at the top of the list of features to include in the backyard play space. Swings have existed such a long time that much is now known about their use and proper design.

The best-known fact is that all children jump out of swings—it is as close to flying as they can get. Unfortunately, jumping out of swings can lead to injuries. The likelihood of accidents will be considerably reduced if a clear space with soft ground cover extends out from both the front and rear of the swing, two times the height of the swing beam. The swing beam itself should not be higher than eight feet above ground. Greater heights increase the potential for injury. A tire swing, which cannot be pumped back and forth easily but swings in all directions, is fun for children and reduces the temptation to jump.

Swing frame

Chapter 2 integrates swings with structures; here the swings are free-standing on separate frames. The most critical safety component of any swing is its frame. It must be sturdy enough to withstand the enormous force generated by an exuberantly swinging child—so build the frame carefully and well.

The beam must be long enough so a child will not hit one of the legs and strong enough to support the load. Two to-and-fro swings require a 12-foot beam made of a 4 by 6 or two laminated 2 by 6s. A 16-foot beam that extends beyond the legs for bracing is recommended for the tire swing, which several children can play on at the same time.

This heavy beam and the side-to-side forces generated by swinging require rigid uprights for support. Uprights are generally constructed as A-frames for maximum strength. Because A-frames can require skillful carpentry to construct, another method uses massive end posts—6 by 6s or double 4 by 4s.

All the lumber for the projects should be pressure-treated or painted with preservative to resist rot and insect damage. When the project is finished, it can be painted with high-grade gloss enamel. To maintain the appearance of the natural wood, spray or brush with a quality water-repellent sealer. For the best water repellent, look for a product that meets Federal Specification TT-W-572B. See page 35, "Protecting wood from decay," for more information on the subject.

Because swing frames are subject to considerable stress, they should be

Figure A   The A-frame swing

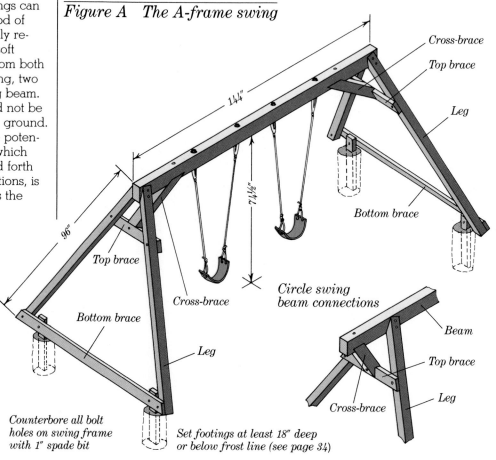

Cross-brace

Top brace

Leg

Bottom brace

Top brace

Cross-brace

Bottom brace

Leg

144"

96"

7'4½"

Circle swing beam connections

Beam

Top brace

Leg

Cross-brace

Counterbore all bolt holes on swing frame with 1" spade bit

Set footings at least 18" deep or below frost line (see page 34)

inspected at least every two months. Test footings to be certain they are secure. Check wood for rot. Examine rope, seat, and top connections. Check nuts and bolts that hold the unit together to be sure they are tight.

Of the two ways described here to support the swing beam, the A-frame is structurally stronger. The double post is strong enough if it is anchored to the ground with proper footings (footings for various soils and climate conditions are discussed on pages 34–35). Tire swings also require sturdier bracing than to-and-fro swings to withstand side-to-side stress.

Build the A-frame swing

The tools needed to build any of the three A-frame swings include saw, protractor, bevel square or try square or combination square, 25-foot tape rule, hand or electric drill with a ½-inch auger bit and a 1-inch spade bit, ⁹/₁₆-inch socket wrench, and posthole digger. Have a helper on hand.

Buy lumber and hardware. Select straight boards that are dry and as free as possible from cracks, checks, and knots. Lay out each piece of lumber and make all necessary cuts (follow illustrations on the right).

Materials list
To-and-fro swing

4x6 treated lumber
1 piece 144″ long for beam

4x4 treated lumber
4 pieces 96″ long for legs
2 pieces 31″ long for cross-braces
4 pieces cut to length for footings:
    See pages 34–35 on "Footings"

2x4 treated lumber
2 pieces 93″ long for bottom braces
2 pieces 31″ long for top braces

Hardware and miscellaneous
2 carriage bolts ⅜″x4″; nuts, washers
18 carriage bolts ⅜″x5″; nuts, washers
2 carriage bolts ⅜″x6½″; nuts, washers
4 carriage bolts ⅜″x8″; nuts, washers
48 galvanized common nails 16d

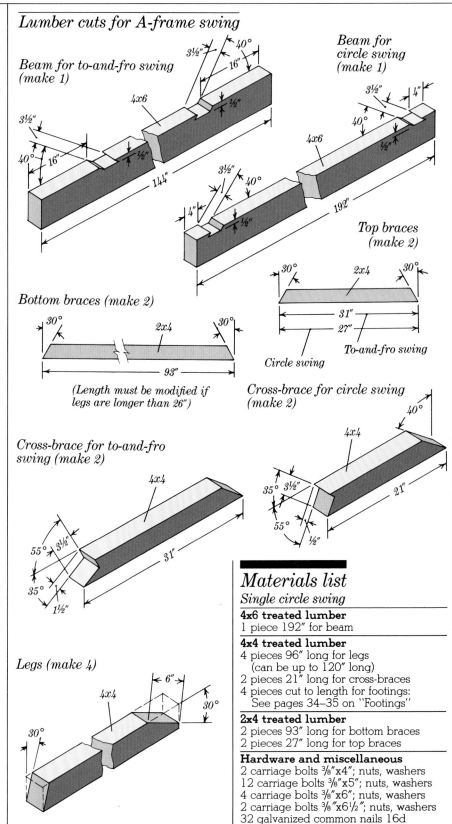

Lumber cuts for A-frame swing

Beam for to-and-fro swing (make 1)

Beam for circle swing (make 1)

Bottom braces (make 2)

(Length must be modified if legs are longer than 26″)

Top braces (make 2)

To-and-fro swing

Circle swing

Cross-brace for to-and-fro swing (make 2)

Cross-brace for circle swing (make 2)

Legs (make 4)

Materials list
Single circle swing

4x6 treated lumber
1 piece 192″ for beam

4x4 treated lumber
4 pieces 96″ long for legs
    (can be up to 120″ long)
2 pieces 21″ long for cross-braces
4 pieces cut to length for footings:
    See pages 34–35 on "Footings"

2x4 treated lumber
2 pieces 93″ long for bottom braces
2 pieces 27″ long for top braces

Hardware and miscellaneous
2 carriage bolts ⅜″x4″; nuts, washers
12 carriage bolts ⅜″x5″; nuts, washers
4 carriage bolts ⅜″x6″; nuts, washers
2 carriage bolts ⅜″x6½″; nuts, washers
32 galvanized common nails 16d

Swings

Place two legs on the ground. Lay top and bottom braces across legs in the proper position (Figure B-1). Drill two ½-inch-diameter holes at each end of each brace. Make ½-inch-deep counterbores on the back of legs with a 1-inch spade bit. Bolt braces loosely in place.

Ask helper to hold one leg assembly upright while you slide beam into position (at the end for to-and-fro swing frame and 24 inches from the end for circle swing frame). Use the protractor to position beam at a 105-degree angle to leg assembly (Figure B-2). Another method is to measure 73 inches from end of beam, make a mark, then move leg until bottom end is 10 feet from mark. This will be close enough to 105 degrees.

Make two ½-inch-deep counterbores with a 1-inch spade bit in top of legs. With a ½-inch auger bit, drill two ½-inch-diameter holes through top of legs and beam as shown in Figure B-3 or B-4. Bolt leg assembly loosely in place.

Put cross-brace in position. Drill holes, and counterbore for beam and top-brace connections (see Figure B-3 or B-4). Bolt loosely in place.

Now tighten all bolts securely. The ⅜-inch bolts in ½-inch holes should leave enough adjustment for measurements and lumber sizes that are not quite accurate.

Repeat leg assembly instructions for second A-frame. Stand frame upright and position in its permanent location.

Use posthole digger to dig footing holes as deep as necessary for your area (see pages 34–35). The add-on footings, shown in Figure A, are described on page 34.

When soil is firmly tamped or concrete is set, tighten bolts. Then hang the swings of your choice.

Figure B A-frame swing construction

Figure B-1

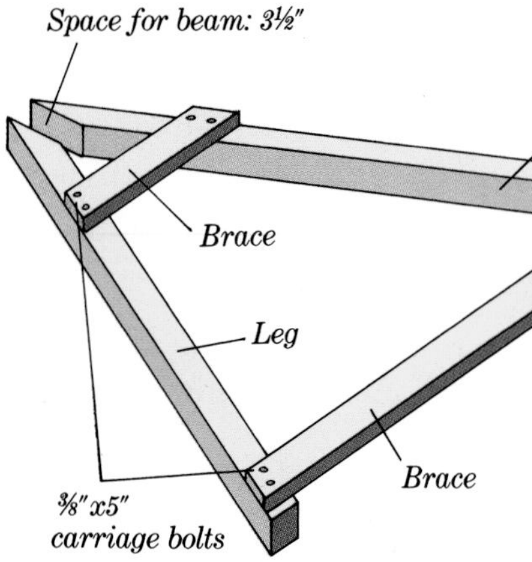

Space for beam: 3½"
Leg
Brace
Leg
Brace
⅜"x5" carriage bolts

Figure B-2

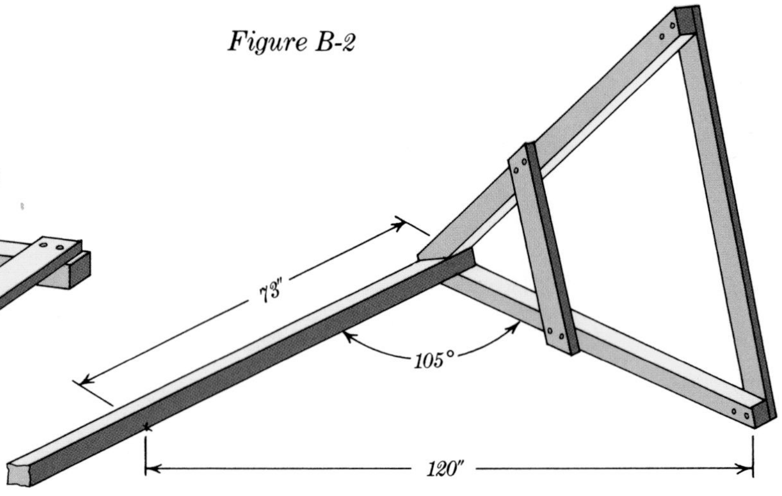

73"
105°
120"

Figure B-4 Circle swing

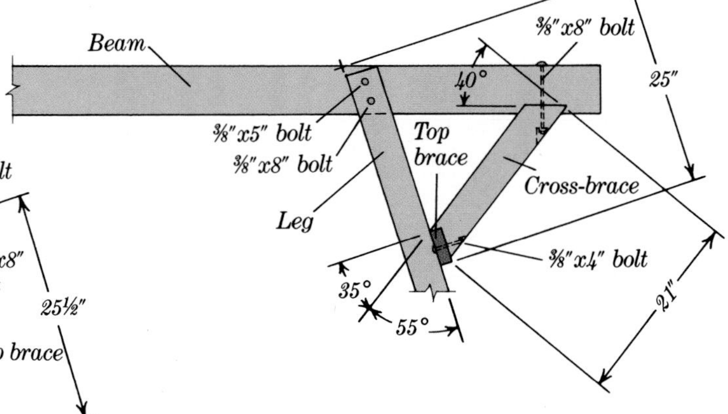

Beam
⅜"x8" bolt
40°
25"
⅜"x5" bolt
⅜"x8" bolt
Top brace
Cross-brace
Leg
⅜"x4" bolt
35°
55°
21"

Figure B-3 To-and-fro swing

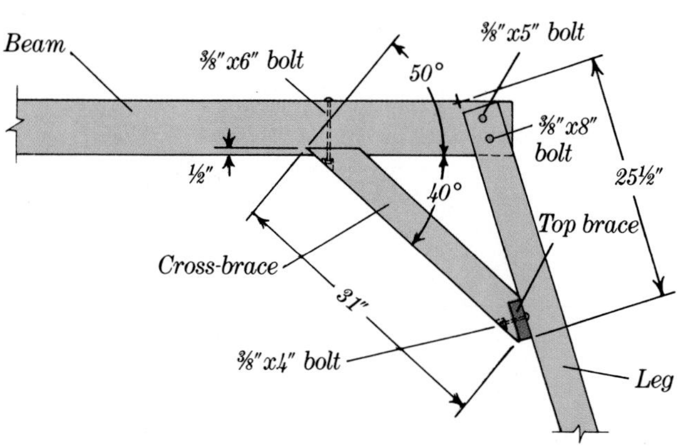

Beam
⅜"x6" bolt
50°
⅜"x5" bolt
⅜"x8" bolt
½"
40°
25½"
Top brace
Cross-brace
31"
⅜"x4" bolt
Leg

All bolts are carriage bolts and require ½" counterbore with 1" spade bit

Post-and-beam frame

This post-and-beam frame is not as rigid as the A-frame, although it is quite a bit easier to build. It is recommended for a single swing only and must be set in rather massive concrete footings that extend to or below frost line (see pages 34–35).

Tools needed include saw, carpenter's steel square, 25-foot tape rule, hand or electric drill with a ½-inch auger bit and a 1-inch spade bit, ⁹/₁₆-inch socket wrench, posthole digger, shovel, hammer, and carpenter's level.

Buy lumber and hardware after determining desired height of swing and necessary depth of footings. Cut any pieces, the 24-inch spacers, for instance, that were not cut to size at the lumberyard.

Lay all pieces in position (see Figure C). Use a square to make sure corners are true. Drill all holes with a ½-inch auger bit. Using a 1-inch spade bit, drill a 1-inch-deep counterbore for each hole. Bolt all pieces together.

Dig holes for posts at least 16 inches in diameter and as deep as the frost line in your area (see pages 34–35 for more information on footings).

Stand frame upright and brace it level with scrap boards and stakes, as shown in Figure C-1.

Mix concrete according to directions and pour into holes. Tamp to remove bubbles. When concrete is set, attach swing.

Materials list
Post-and-beam swing

2x6 treated lumber
1 piece 96″ long for beam

4x4 treated lumber
4 pieces 96″ to 120″ long for posts:
See "Footings" on pages 34–35

2x4 treated lumber
4 pieces 24″ long for spacers

Hardware and miscellaneous
12 carriage bolts ⅜″x8″; washers, nuts
24 galvanized common nails 16d
Ready-mixed concrete: See "Footings" on pages 34–35 for amount needed

---

Figure C   Post-and-beam swing

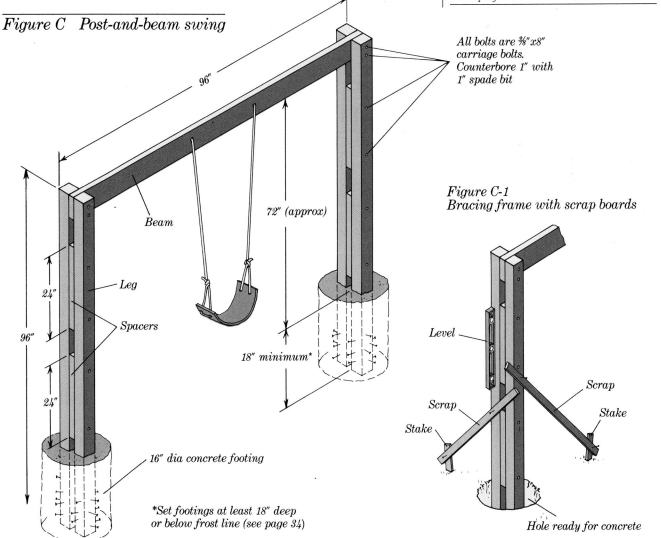

All bolts are ⅜″x8″ carriage bolts. Counterbore 1″ with 1″ spade bit

96″

72″ (approx)

Beam

Leg

Spacers

24″

96″

24″

18″ minimum*

16″ dia concrete footing

*Set footings at least 18″ deep or below frost line (see page 34)

Figure C-1
Bracing frame with scrap boards

Level

Scrap

Scrap

Stake

Stake

Hole ready for concrete

Swing attachments

Swing-frame attachments

Always select play equipment for children with safety in mind. For instance, the swing seat that is most comfortable and easiest to make consists of a simple board. Sometimes, however, children toss the seat around, which can lead to head injuries. To avoid this possibility, we recommend that you make the swing seat from a tire tread or buy a ready-made flexible seat. If you still prefer to make a board swing, make it from a lightweight wood such as pine or redwood, and round off all corners and edges.

Because public playground swings must be vandalproof, steel chain is used for support. For the home, high-grade nylon or polypropylene rope is adequate. Several ways are shown to attach rope to swing and frame. Remember rope-to-rope, rope-to-wood, or rope-to-metal connections cause wear on the rope. These connections must be checked every month or so to be sure that they remain safe.

The simplest rope-to-frame connection is made by drilling a hole a little larger than the rope, threading the rope through, and tying a stevedore knot at the end to hold it. You

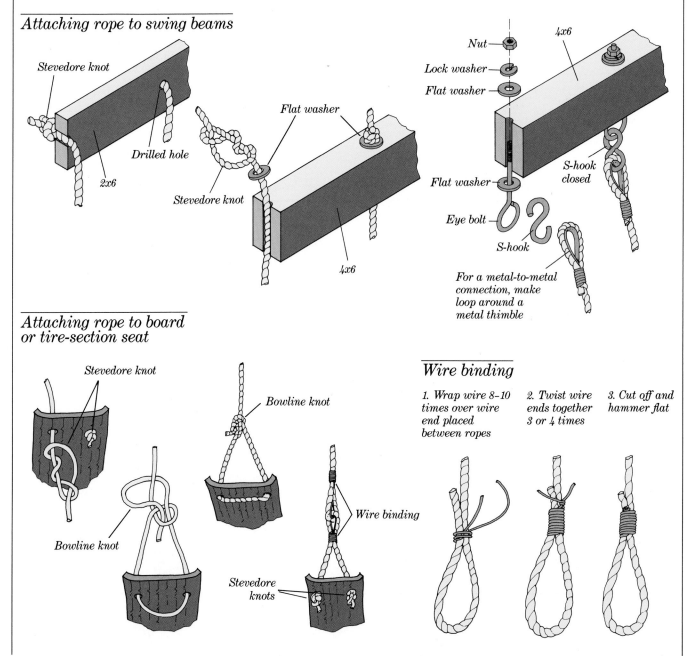

Attaching rope to swing beams

Stevedore knot
Drilled hole
2x6

Flat washer
Stevedore knot
4x6

Nut
Lock washer
Flat washer
4x6
S-hook closed
Flat washer
Eye bolt
S-hook
For a metal-to-metal connection, make loop around a metal thimble

Attaching rope to board or tire-section seat

Stevedore knot
Bowline knot
Bowline knot
Wire binding
Stevedore knots

Wire binding

1. Wrap wire 8–10 times over wire end placed between ropes

2. Twist wire ends together 3 or 4 times

3. Cut off and hammer flat

can drill a vertical hole in a 4-by beam, but in a 2 by 6 or 2 by 8, a vertical hole will weaken the beam too much. Drill the hole horizontally on 2-by beams.

When a rope is looped through an eye bolt, swing seat, or other part, it can be secured with a simple bowline knot, or by wire binding. The latter is much neater and cannot be unfastened by curious children.

Commercial bearings for connecting rope or chain to beam—available at large hardware or playground supply outlets—are safe and easy to use. Several homemade bearings are shown here. Use metal thimbles in rope loops whenever possible, and forged or hardened eye bolts, S-hooks, and other metal parts when you can find them. Metal-to-metal connections can wear through in a

few months of heavy activity, so inspect these frequently.

Circle swings, made from a tire, a Frisbee™, or a sawdust-filled burlap sack, are fun for children of all ages, even those too young to pump a to-and-fro swing. A tire may be hung upright or flat but flat is best. Children seem to like the flat tire better because more than one child can spin around on it at the same time.

Various swings

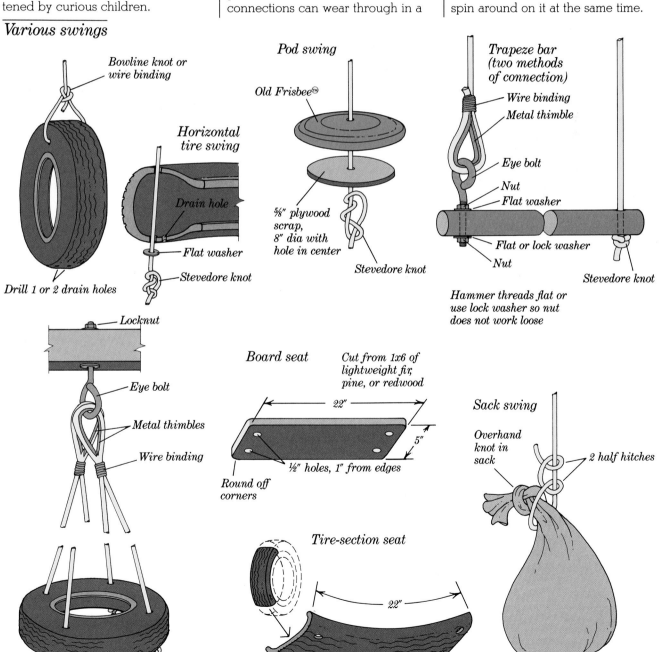

Bowline knot or wire binding

Pod swing

Old Frisbee™

Trapeze bar
(two methods of connection)

Wire binding
Metal thimble

Horizontal tire swing

Eye bolt
Nut
Flat washer

Drain hole

⅝" plywood scrap, 8" dia with hole in center

Flat washer
Stevedore knot

Stevedore knot

Flat or lock washer
Nut

Drill 1 or 2 drain holes

Stevedore knot

Hammer threads flat or use lock washer so nut does not work loose

Locknut

Eye bolt

Metal thimbles

Wire binding

Board seat

Cut from 1x6 of lightweight fir, pine, or redwood

22"

5"

½" holes, 1" from edges

Round off corners

Sack swing

Overhand knot in sack

2 half hitches

Tire-section seat

22"

23

SLIDES

Of the many types of slides, the traditional straight slide and the wave slide are favorites with children.

Use treated lumber for these projects. They can be painted with quality gloss enamel or, to preserve the appearance of natural wood, sprayed with a good water-repellent sealer. Look for a repellent that meets Federal Specification TT-W-572B.

Straight slide

The materials list shows two sizes for most parts. The two lengths enable the slide to fit on several of the projects in Chapter 2. The top cleat of the longer slide hooks over a cross-member 56 to 58 inches above ground for the Split-level Playhouse (page 81) or to the top rail of the Creative Climber (page 64). The shorter length fits the A-frame Clubhouse (page 41), the Fitness Gym (page 53), or the second rail on the Creative Climber.

Two sizes are also given for the width so you can make a traditional slide or a slide wide enough for two. When you cut materials, be sure that all dimensions are for either long or short, wide or narrow. Tools needed include power saw, electric drill, protractor, square, 12-foot tape rule, jigsaw or saber saw (or belt sander), 7/16-inch auger bit, 1-inch spade bit, No. 1 Phillips screwdriver bit, hammer, router with 1/2-inch roundover bit (or belt sander), two 12-inch bar clamps, and 9/16-inch socket wrench.

Building the straight slide

Buy materials and have sheet metal cut and bent (Figure A). This can usually be done at sheet-metal or heating and air-conditioning outlets.

Cut plywood to size. Starting 14 1/2-inches from the end, make 12 cuts across, 1/2 inch apart and 1/4 inch deep (Figure B).

Soak parallel cuts in water—or pile with sopping rags—for 24 hours.

Cut four 2 by 4 side rails (Figures C and D). With a protractor, mark 28-degree angles at one end of each upper side rail. Draw curve on lower side rails (Figure C). Cut angles and curves. If you do not have a jigsaw or saber saw, you can shape the curve with a rasp or belt sander.

Assemble upper and lower side rails (Figure D). Clamp pieces together and drill holes through both pieces with 7/16-inch auger bit. Drill 1/2-inch-deep counterbores on bottom of lower side rail with a 1-inch spade bit. Put a line of waterproof glue on joints and bolt pieces tightly together.

After plywood has soaked for 24 hours, position two side rails with bottom sides up (Figure E). Lay sheet metal on top of rails, and place plywood on sheet metal so parallel cuts are over curve, and ends of plywood are inserted in bent ends of metal. Position pieces so sharp edges of metal are inset 1/8 inch inside edges of plywood and rails.

Secure plywood and metal to rails with 2 1/2-inch galvanized multipurpose screws every 6 inches (Figure F). Start screw through plywood and metal with a hammer, tighten with an electric drill and screwdriver bit. Add four extra screws at the curve.

Position legs against rails 6 inches from bottom end of slide (Figure G). Drill holes through both legs and

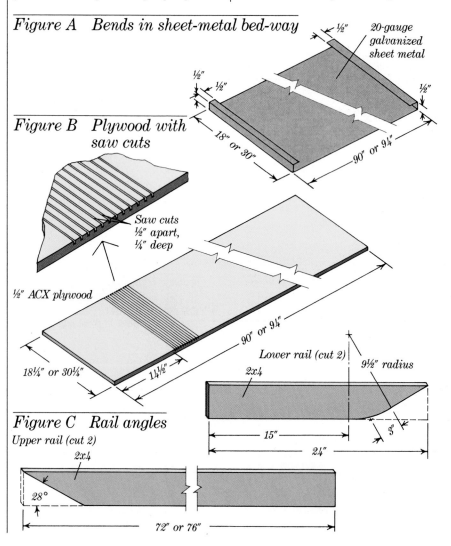

Figure A   Bends in sheet-metal bed-way

1/2"
20-gauge galvanized sheet metal
1/2"
1/2"
1/2"
1/2"
18" or 30"
90" or 94"

Figure B   Plywood with saw cuts

Saw cuts 1/2" apart, 1/4" deep

1/2" ACX plywood

90" or 94"

18 1/4" or 30 1/4"
11 1/2"

Figure C   Rail angles

Lower rail (cut 2)
2x4
9 1/2" radius
15"
3"
24"

Upper rail (cut 2)
2x4
28°
72" or 76"

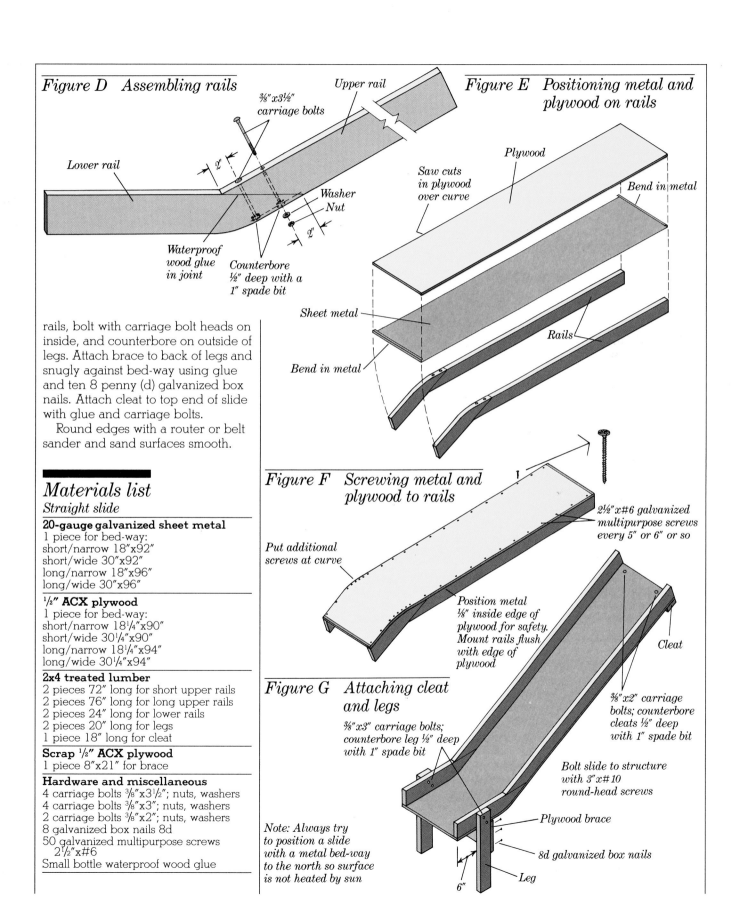

Figure D   Assembling rails

⅜"x3½" carriage bolts

Upper rail

Lower rail

2"

Washer
Nut

2"

Waterproof
wood glue
in joint

Counterbore
½" deep with a
1" spade bit

Figure E   Positioning metal and plywood on rails

Plywood

Saw cuts
in plywood
over curve

Bend in metal

Sheet metal

Rails

Bend in metal

Figure F   Screwing metal and plywood to rails

Put additional
screws at curve

2½"x#6 galvanized
multipurpose screws
every 5" or 6" or so

Position metal
⅛" inside edge of
plywood for safety.
Mount rails flush
with edge of
plywood

Cleat

⅜"x2" carriage
bolts; counterbore
cleats ½" deep
with 1" spade bit

Figure G   Attaching cleat and legs

⅜"x3" carriage bolts;
counterbore leg ½" deep
with 1" spade bit

Bolt slide to structure
with 3"x#10
round-head screws

Plywood brace

8d galvanized box nails

Note: Always try
to position a slide
with a metal bed-way
to the north so surface
is not heated by sun

6"

Leg

rails, bolt with carriage bolt heads on inside, and counterbore on outside of legs. Attach brace to back of legs and snugly against bed-way using glue and ten 8 penny (d) galvanized box nails. Attach cleat to top end of slide with glue and carriage bolts.

Round edges with a router or belt sander and sand surfaces smooth.

Materials list
Straight slide

20-gauge galvanized sheet metal
1 piece for bed-way:
short/narrow 18"x92"
short/wide 30"x92"
long/narrow 18"x96"
long/wide 30"x96"

½" ACX plywood
1 piece for bed-way:
short/narrow 18¼"x90"
short/wide 30¼"x90"
long/narrow 18¼"x94"
long/wide 30¼"x94"

2x4 treated lumber
2 pieces 72" long for short upper rails
2 pieces 76" long for long upper rails
2 pieces 24" long for lower rails
2 pieces 20" long for legs
1 piece 18" long for cleat

Scrap ½" ACX plywood
1 piece 8"x21" for brace

Hardware and miscellaneous
4 carriage bolts ⅜"x3½"; nuts, washers
4 carriage bolts ⅜"x3"; nuts, washers
2 carriage bolts ⅜"x2"; nuts, washers
8 galvanized box nails 8d
50 galvanized multipurpose screws
   2½"x#6
Small bottle waterproof wood glue

Slides

Wave slide

This slide is designed to attach to the Split-level Playhouse (page 81). You can cut the rails to follow the waves in the slide or leave them straight. Tools needed to make the wave slide include heavy-duty saber saw, jigsaw, or band saw (or have curves cut at the lumberyard or mill), electric drill with 7/16-inch-long auger bit, 7/16-inch speed bit and 1-inch spade bit, four short bar or pipe clamps, hammer, router with 1/2-inch roundover bit, and 9/16-inch socket wrench.

Building the wave slide

Buy material and have sheet metal cut to size and bent (Figure A). Cut fiberboard to size.

Lay out wave curve on one of the 2 by 12 rails: First draw a grid pattern of 1/2-inch squares on a piece of paper (Figure B). Grid should be 16½ inches long and 3 inches wide, with measurements marked. Designate one end as A and the other B. Make a dot on *your* grid wherever the curve crosses a line on the grid provided. Connect all dots on grid with a smooth curved line, and you have a

template for about 1/7 of the wavy curve. Cut along curve line.

Following Figure C, draw a line down the center of one 2 by 12 board. Lay template on board so centerline of template is on centerline of board. Begin with "A" end of template at "top" end of slide. Trace curve with a pencil.

Turn template over so centerline is on centerline of board, and put "B" end at end of first line and trace curve again. Continue down board until you reach the end.

Draw a 3-inch-long by 1/2-inch-deep notch at each end of rail (Figure D). This is used to reinforce ends of metal bed-way with fiberboard fillers.

Draw the mounting notch at the "top" end, as shown in Figure D.

If you want the rail to follow the wave, draw another curve parallel to the first. Round remaining corners.

Cut along all lines on first 2 by 12

rail with a saber saw, jigsaw, or band saw. Then lay cut rail on uncut one, trace outline, and cut second rail.

If your local lumberyard or mill has a band saw, you may be able to have the rails cut for a small fee.

Nail fiberboard to bottom half of each rail (Figure E). Make four 3-inch by 18-inch fiberboard fillers and tack two in each of the notches at ends.

Lay metal on top of fiberboard with metal edges 1/8 inch inside of the outside edges of fiberboard. This keeps sharp edge of metal safely inside rail. Bend ends of metal hook around ends of fiberboard (Figure F).

Clamp top half of each rail in place with two small bar or pipe clamps. Be sure they line up exactly over bottom halves.

Drill four 7/16-inch holes vertically through each rail, as shown.

Start each hole with speed bit where wood is thinnest. Once you

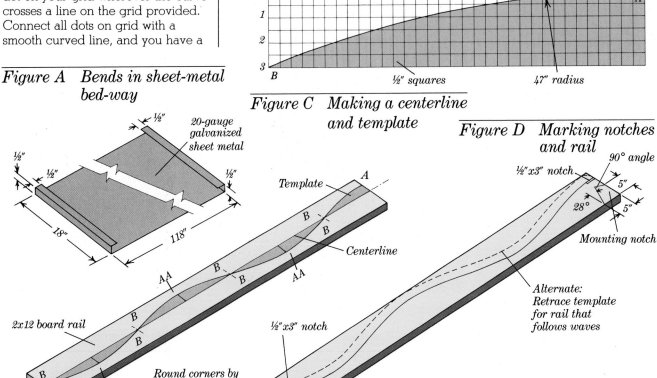

Figure A   Bends in sheet-metal bed-way

20-gauge galvanized sheet metal

2x12 board rail

Figure B   Grid for wave pattern

Inches

½" squares   47" radius

Figure C   Making a centerline and template

Template

Centerline

Round corners by tracing around a coffee or paint can

Figure D   Marking notches and rail

90° angle

½"x3" notch

28°

Mounting notch

½"x3" notch

Alternate: Retrace template for rail that follows waves

are through the metal, switch to auger bit. Position helper to watch that drill remains vertical. It is hard to keep a drill bit centered edgewise through a 2 by 12.

Use 1-inch spade bit to drill a ½-inch-deep countersink at the bottom of each hole.

Bolt rails together; bolt heads on top of rails—nuts in countersinks.

Trim the 2 by 4 braces to fit tightly between rails and against underside of bed-way. Nail in place with 16d nails through the rails.

Cut two 24-inch pieces of 2 by 4 for legs. Use the protractor to position them at bottom end of slide, as shown in Figure G. Drill holes and countersinks; bolt legs in place with heads of carriage bolts on inside of slide.

Use a ½-inch roundover bit in the router to round all edges of slide. Sand thoroughly and finish with gloss enamel or spray with high-grade water-repellent sealer.

Attach slide to Split-level Playhouse with 3-inch wood screws. Drive screws through vertical 2 by 4s of playhouse into sides of slide-rail bottoms.

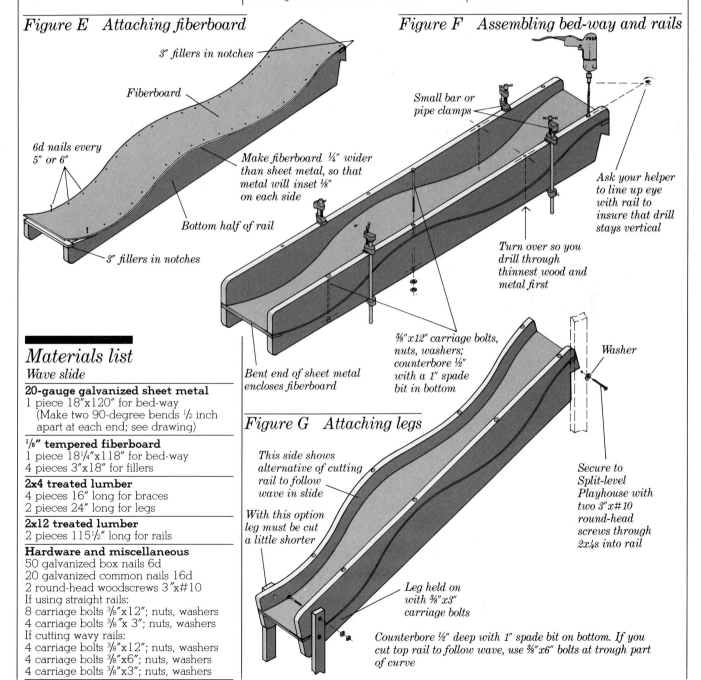

Figure E   Attaching fiberboard

3″ fillers in notches

Fiberboard

6d nails every 5″ or 6″

Make fiberboard ¼″ wider than sheet metal, so that metal will inset ⅛″ on each side

Bottom half of rail

3″ fillers in notches

Figure F   Assembling bed-way and rails

Small bar or pipe clamps

Ask your helper to line up eye with rail to insure that drill stays vertical

Turn over so you drill through thinnest wood and metal first

⅜″ x 12″ carriage bolts, nuts, washers; counterbore ½″ with a 1″ spade bit in bottom

Bent end of sheet metal encloses fiberboard

Washer

Secure to Split-level Playhouse with two 3″ x #10 round-head screws through 2x4s into rail

Figure G   Attaching legs

This side shows alternative of cutting rail to follow wave in slide

With this option leg must be cut a little shorter

Leg held on with ⅜″ x 3″ carriage bolts

Counterbore ½″ deep with 1″ spade bit on bottom. If you cut top rail to follow wave, use ⅜″ x 6″ bolts at trough part of curve

Materials list
Wave slide

20-gauge galvanized sheet metal
1 piece 18″x120″ for bed-way
(Make two 90-degree bends ½ inch apart at each end; see drawing)

⅛″ tempered fiberboard
1 piece 18¼″x118″ for bed-way
4 pieces 3″x18″ for fillers

2x4 treated lumber
4 pieces 16″ long for braces
2 pieces 24″ long for legs

2x12 treated lumber
2 pieces 115½″ long for rails

Hardware and miscellaneous
50 galvanized box nails 6d
20 galvanized common nails 16d
2 round-head woodscrews 3″x#10
If using straight rails:
8 carriage bolts ⅜″x12″; nuts, washers
4 carriage bolts ⅜″x 3″; nuts, washers
If cutting wavy rails:
4 carriage bolts ⅜″x12″; nuts, washers
4 carriage bolts ⅜″x6″; nuts, washers
4 carriage bolts ⅜″x3″; nuts, washers

FITNESS COMPONENTS

*I*n the past several years, physical fitness has become one of the most popular avocations in the United States. What started out as a fad ten years ago has grown to be a way of life for many people. Running, rowing, aerobic classes, fitness gyms, and home fitness centers have all become commonplace.

Many public parks and jogging trails incorporate exercise centers or exercise stations. These exercise trails not only alleviate the boredom of jogging, but add strength, flexibility, balance, and confidence of movement to the endurance gained by running.

Much of the apparatus usually found along exercise courses and in fitness centers is incorporated in the larger projects in Chapter 2 of this book. The following projects allow you to add other stations to those

projects or build the exercise apparatus by itself. These eight projects give you all the stations needed for a full exercise trail.

Some of these projects can be combined to save materials and work time. Five of the projects call for two 4 by 4 posts. For example, if two projects are built side-by-side, they can share one post. It is inadvisable, however, to use the same two posts for more than one project—the rings and chin-up bars, for instance. If you had to remove the bar to use the rings or vice versa, the continuity of the exercise circuit would be broken and some of the aerobic benefit lost.

If people of different heights or abilities will be using the equipment, you might want to add a post to allow for chinning bars at two levels.

The following are some of the standard exercises that can be performed on each of these projects. We do not, however, show or recommend how these exercises should be performed, what kind of condition you should be

in, and what kind of warm-up is necessary to do them safely. Before doing any exercise, see your doctor, and learn how to exercise properly from a qualified coach or a good book on the subject. *The Exer-Trail Way to Total Fitness* by Dr. James R. Tiffany and Robert A. Moss, published by Leisure Press, New York, is a book that shows specifically how to use this kind of equipment.

The following projects do not have individual materials lists, instead, the illustrations show all materials necessary for the projects.

The board

A 2 by 12 board, 6 feet long with a cleat at each end and a handle at one end, can be used by itself for leg-ups, bent-knee sit-ups, sit-and-reaches, body curls, lateral arm raises, and butterfly stretches.

By propping the handle end on the low bar, it can be used for more difficult leg raises, bent-knee sit-ups, and body curls. Set it next to one of the step-up posts for leg raises over the post.

The board

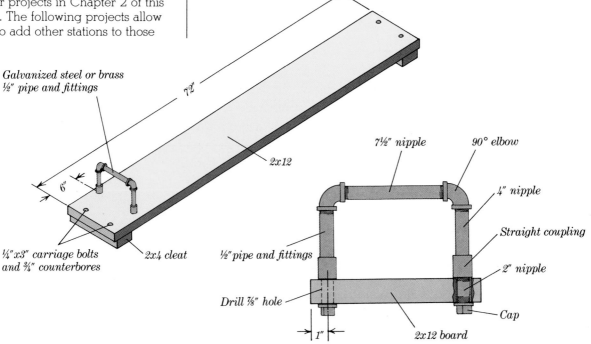

Galvanized steel or brass ½" pipe and fittings

7'2"

6"

2x12

¼"x3" carriage bolts and ¾" counterbores

2x4 cleat

7½" nipple

90° elbow

4" nipple

Straight coupling

2" nipple

Cap

½" pipe and fittings

Drill ⅞" hole

1"

2x12 board

Step-up posts

This is a series of posts that extend from 12 inches to 24 inches above ground. They can be made from either 6 by 6s or 6-inch-diameter wood "legs." By themselves, they can be used for step up–step down exercises, which require that you step up with one foot, bring the other foot up, then step down again, gradually moving to higher and higher posts. In conjunction with the board, they can be used for leg raises over the posts.

Low bar

The low bar can be adjusted for various functions and abilities. By itself, the bar can be used for push-ups, body lifts, static stretches and bent-knee stretches. Hook the cleat of the board on the pipe bar to give it a slant for bent-knee sit-ups, leg-ups, and body curls.

Rings

The rings can be used for hip circles and pull-ups. The posts can be used for Achilles tendon stretches and for vertical jumps.

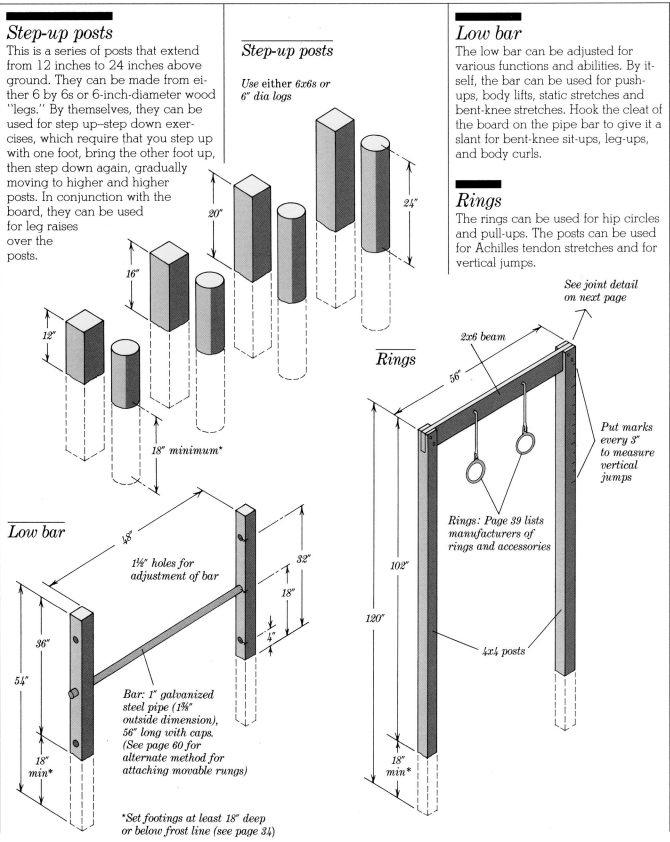

Step-up posts

Use either *6x6s* or *6" dia logs*

20"

16"

24"

12"

18" *minimum**

Rings

See joint detail on next page

2x6 beam

56"

Put marks every 3" to measure vertical jumps

Rings: Page 39 lists manufacturers of rings and accessories

102"

120"

4x4 posts

18" min*

Low bar

48"

32"

18"

4"

1½" holes for adjustment of bar

36"

54"

18" min*

Bar: 1" galvanized steel pipe (1⅜" outside dimension), 56" long with caps. (See page 60 for alternate method for attaching movable rungs)

*Set footings at least 18" deep or below frost line (see page 34)

Fitness Components

Parallel bars

This device is designed for the parallel bar walk—holding one's weight above the bars with straight arms and walking with hands down the length of the bar—and bar dips—raising and lowering one's body with hands on bars and weight supported by arms. The rungs on the ends can be used with the board for bent-knee sit-ups, leg-ups, and body curls.

Horizontal ladder

The horizontal ladder is designed for swinging from rung to rung but can also be used for chin-ups and pull-ups if you are careful not to bump your head on adjoining rungs. The rungs on the vertical posts can hold the board at a slant for bent-knee sit-ups, leg-ups, and body curls. Any of the vertical posts is suitable for Achilles tendon stretches.

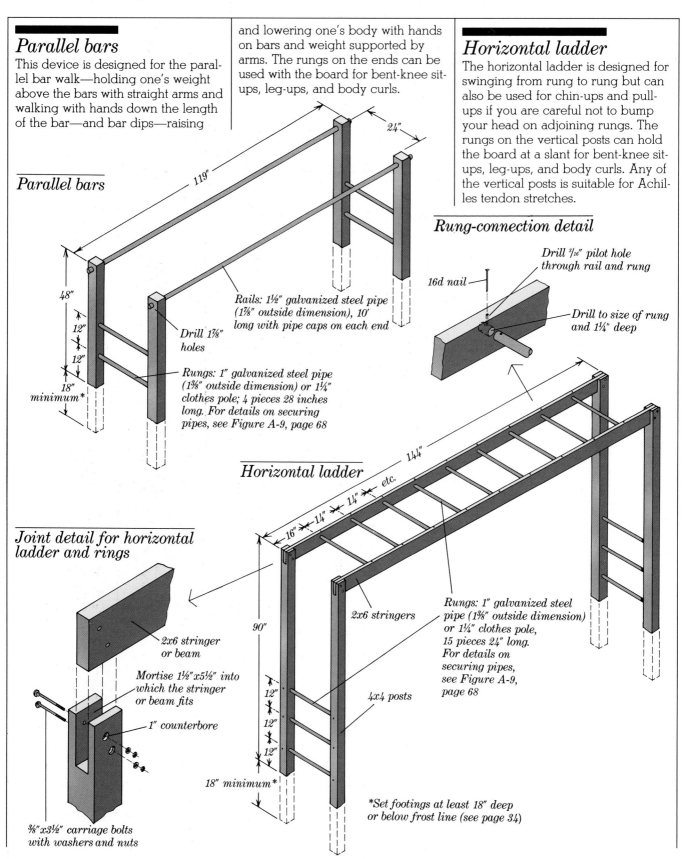

Parallel bars

24"

119"

48"

12"

12"

18" minimum*

Drill 1⅛" holes

Rails: 1½" galvanized steel pipe (1⅞" outside dimension), 10' long with pipe caps on each end

Rungs: 1" galvanized steel pipe (1⅜" outside dimension) or 1¼" clothes pole; 4 pieces 28 inches long. For details on securing pipes, see Figure A-9, page 68

Rung-connection detail

Drill ³⁄₁₆" pilot hole through rail and rung

16d nail

Drill to size of rung and 1¼" deep

Joint detail for horizontal ladder and rings

2x6 stringer or beam

Mortise 1½"x5½" into which the stringer or beam fits

1" counterbore

⅜"x3½" carriage bolts with washers and nuts

Horizontal ladder

144"

16" 1⅛" 1⅛" 1⅛" etc.

90"

12"

12"

12"

18" minimum*

2x6 stringers

4x4 posts

Rungs: 1" galvanized steel pipe (1⅜" outside dimension) or 1¼" clothes pole, 15 pieces 24" long. For details on securing pipes, see Figure A-9, page 68

*Set footings at least 18" deep or below frost line (see page 34)

Sandbox/balance beam

Build a below-grade sandbox (see page 33) with taller, uncapped 2-bys on 2 sides for balance beam

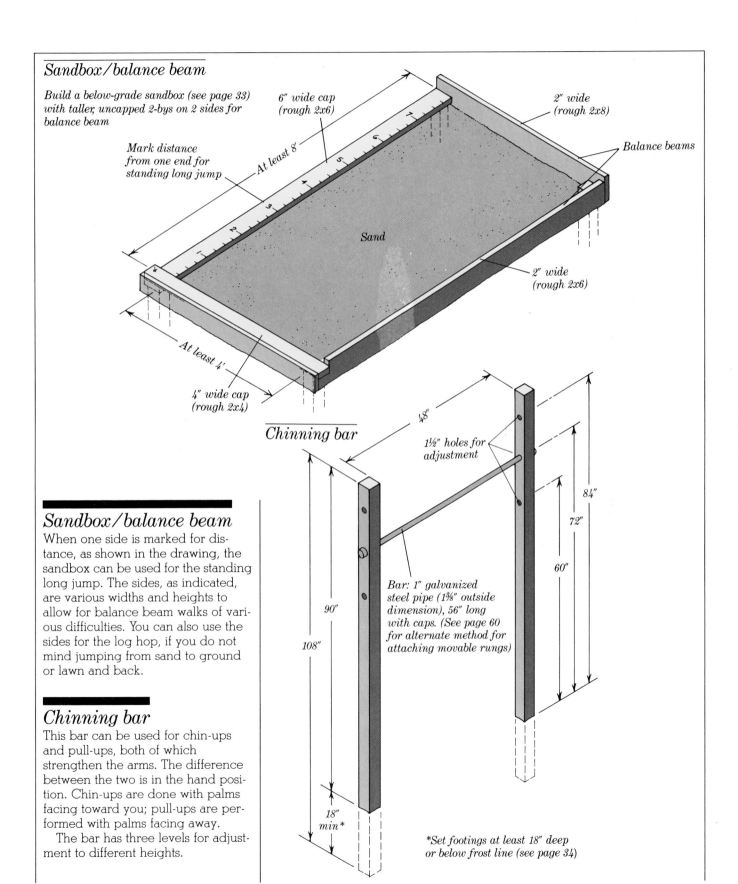

6" wide cap (rough 2x6)

2" wide (rough 2x8)

Balance beams

Mark distance from one end for standing long jump

At least 8'

Sand

2" wide (rough 2x6)

At least 4'

4" wide cap (rough 2x4)

Chinning bar

48"

1½" holes for adjustment

84"

72"

60"

Bar: 1" galvanized steel pipe (1⅜" outside dimension), 56" long with caps. (See page 60 for alternate method for attaching movable rungs)

90"

108"

18" min*

*Set footings at least 18" deep or below frost line (see page 34)

Sandbox/balance beam

When one side is marked for distance, as shown in the drawing, the sandbox can be used for the standing long jump. The sides, as indicated, are various widths and heights to allow for balance beam walks of various difficulties. You can also use the sides for the log hop, if you do not mind jumping from sand to ground or lawn and back.

Chinning bar

This bar can be used for chin-ups and pull-ups, both of which strengthen the arms. The difference between the two is in the hand position. Chin-ups are done with palms facing toward you; pull-ups are performed with palms facing away.

The bar has three levels for adjustment to different heights.

SANDBOXES

*C*omplexity is not necessary for a successful play area. For example, sandboxes are very simple, but children truly enjoy them.

Even though parents know how much children enjoy a sandbox, they often restrict access because they want to avoid the resulting mess. You can design the play area to reduce this problem.

High-quality, large-grained sand that has been washed before delivery will be much less trouble than dirty, fine-grained sand that produces mud when mixed with water.

If there are cats in the neighborhood, the sandbox needs a cover. A hinged trapdoor of plywood or chicken wire on a 1 by 3 frame is a recommended solution. Toy stores have small plastic or wooden sandboxes with umbrellalike covers that can be raised to provide shade. The tricky part about the sandbox cover is remembering to put it on at the end of the day.

Building a sandbox

If you want a relatively large sandbox that is a part of the landscaping, there are two basic methods: Build a retaining wall of wood or masonry to confine the sand or dig a shallow hole in the ground and fill it with sand, like a sand trap or bunker on a golf course. The retaining wall can be above or below grade and made of railroad ties or 2-by lumber.

Railroad ties are treated with creosote to prevent rot and insect damage. Creosote stains clothing and can cause skin irritation. If you use ties, put a cap of untreated Douglas fir on top for a seat. Round the edges and sand smooth. This keeps children from sitting on or coming into direct contact with the ties.

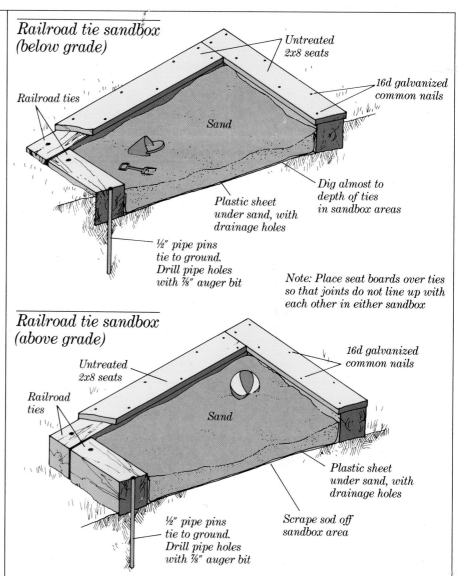

Railroad tie sandbox (below grade)

Untreated 2x8 seats

16d galvanized common nails

Railroad ties

Sand

Dig almost to depth of ties in sandbox areas

Plastic sheet under sand, with drainage holes

½" pipe pins tie to ground. Drill pipe holes with ⅞" auger bit

Note: Place seat boards over ties so that joints do not line up with each other in either sandbox

Railroad tie sandbox (above grade)

Untreated 2x8 seats

16d galvanized common nails

Railroad ties

Sand

Plastic sheet under sand, with drainage holes

½" pipe pins tie to ground. Drill pipe holes with ⅞" auger bit

Scrape sod off sandbox area

If you use 2-bys and posts, select pressure-treated lumber or redwood for the posts and boards that make contact with the sand and soil. Again, put a seat of untreated Douglas fir on top so children avoid touching treated lumber or picking up redwood splinters.

The hole and berm method is simple. Just pull dirt from the sandbox area to form a mound around the edge. If the sand is to be placed within the lawn, skin sod from area, dig hole, and pile dirt around the edge. Then cover dirt mound with sod, and the border will look as if it has been there all along. Sometimes simply piling sod around the perimeter creates a berm with a sufficiently high border.

To keep sand clean and to discourage burrowing animals, line bottom of sandbox with polyethylene sheeting. Poke several small drainage holes in the sheeting.

Several methods of wood construction are shown here. Additional methods and materials for building retaining walls and edgings can be found in other Ortho books: *Ortho's Home Improvement Encyclopedia, Garden Construction, How to Design & Build Decks & Patios,* and *Basic Masonry Techniques.*

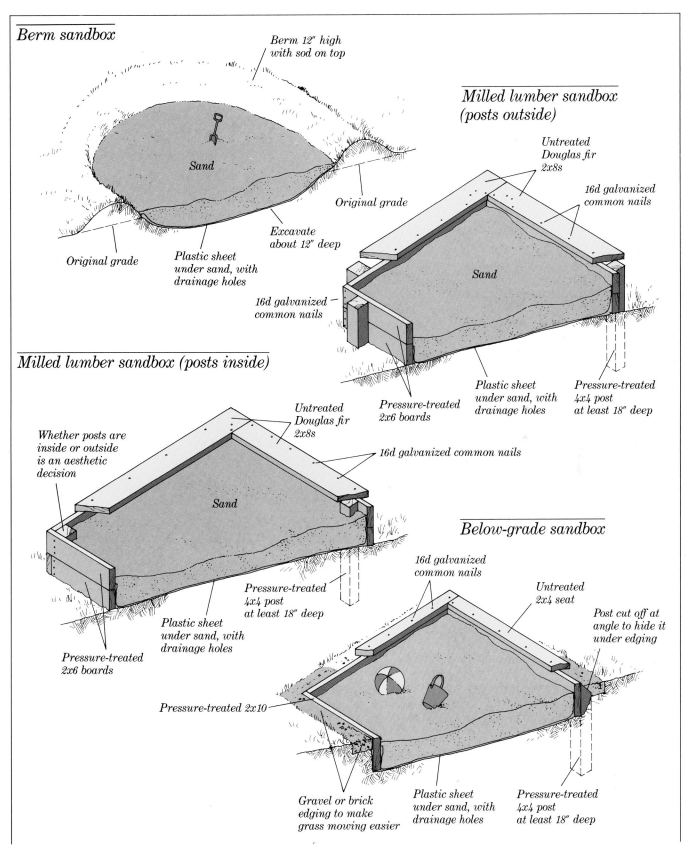

Berm sandbox

Berm 12" high
with sod on top

Sand

Original grade

Original grade

Plastic sheet
under sand, with
drainage holes

Excavate
about 12" deep

**Milled lumber sandbox
(posts outside)**

Untreated
Douglas fir
2x8s

16d galvanized
common nails

Sand

16d galvanized
common nails

Pressure-treated
2x6 boards

Plastic sheet
under sand, with
drainage holes

Pressure-treated
4x4 post
at least 18" deep

Milled lumber sandbox (posts inside)

Whether posts are
inside or outside
is an aesthetic
decision

Untreated
Douglas fir
2x8s

16d galvanized common nails

Sand

Pressure-treated
4x4 post
at least 18" deep

Plastic sheet
under sand, with
drainage holes

Pressure-treated
2x6 boards

Below-grade sandbox

16d galvanized
common nails

Untreated
2x4 seat

Post cut off at
angle to hide it
under edging

Pressure-treated 2x10

Gravel or brick
edging to make
grass mowing easier

Plastic sheet
under sand, with
drainage holes

Pressure-treated
4x4 post
at least 18" deep

Footings

A footing is the means by which a construction is connected to the ground. For the projects in this book, the purpose of footings is to keep play or exercise equipment upright, stable, and securely rooted to its appointed location.

Some of the equipment has only one or two legs and must be secured to the ground to stand up at all. Other projects have three, four, or more legs and can stand by themselves, but need to be anchored so they will not wobble or "walk" when children are swinging, jumping, and applying other forces.

In either case, the construction of the footing is the same. Depth, lumber size, and amount of concrete may vary from project to project, but the components and their relationships do not. A footing for all the projects in this book consists of: a wood post and several 16 penny (d) or 20d galvanized common nails or a post anchor, a hole in the ground, and ready-mixed concrete.

Frost heave

If you live on the West or Gulf coasts of the United States, you need not worry about frost heave. But if you live where the temperature drops below 32° F for extended periods in the winter, it is an important concern.

When moisture in the ground freezes, it expands and causes the surface and anything embedded in it to heave. Fence posts, building foundations, and footings are pushed out of alignment, sometimes even up and out of the ground, during successive freezes and thaws.

The frost line is an imaginary line at the maximum depth to which the freezing extends in any given area. Each city and county has established the frost line for its jurisdiction. The building code for Glen Gardner, New Jersey, for instance, specifies that footings must be 3 feet deep. To determine your frost line, contact your local building inspector or the office for building permits.

The post

When the post that goes into the ground is part of the apparatus, its thickness is designated in the materials list—usually a 4 by 4. Do not change this size according to what you read here. When the footing post is a separate piece used only to anchor the project, a 2 by 4 is adequate, although you can use a 4 by 4 if scrap pieces are available. The post must be long enough to connect securely to the apparatus above ground and to reach at least 18 inches below ground. In areas where frost heave occurs, the post must go deep enough to meet or exceed frost line, or it must be bolted to a post anchor embedded in concrete that does.

Any wood placed below ground must be protected from rot and insects. Pressure-treated lumber is best (see pages 35–36 for information on pressure-treated wood). Short of that, use rot-resistant wood such as redwood or cedar, and be sure to soak it thoroughly in a wood preservative. Even treated wood benefits from an additional rolled or sprayed application of high-quality sealer.

Before setting post into hole, drive three or four 16d or 20d nails halfway into each face where post will be embedded in concrete. This keeps post secure even if it should dry out a little and shrink within the concrete.

Post anchors

A post anchor is a metal device for securing a 4 by 4 post to concrete. The U-shaped or zigzag extension on the anchor is set into fresh concrete. Then the post is bolted or nailed to the sides of the anchor.

These anchors can be used anytime in place of a wood anchor, but they are recommended when frost line makes using wood impractical.

The hole

As with the post, the hole must be at least 18 inches deep or to the frost line, whichever is deeper. The diameter of the hole for a 2 by 4 or 4 by 4 post can be 8 inches or larger. A standard posthole digger makes an 8-inch hole.

Basic footing

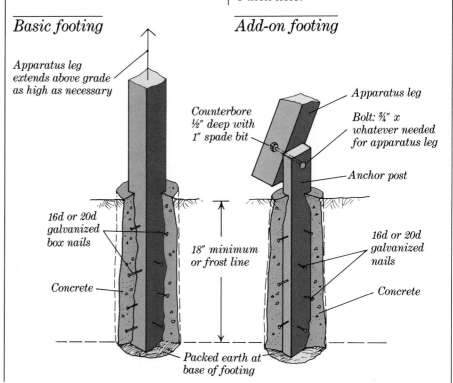

Apparatus leg extends above grade as high as necessary

16d or 20d galvanized box nails

18" minimum or frost line

Concrete

Packed earth at base of footing

Add-on footing

Counterbore ½" deep with 1" spade bit

Apparatus leg

Bolt: ¾" x whatever needed for apparatus leg

Anchor post

16d or 20d galvanized nails

Concrete

To anchor swings, rings, or any apparatus that tends to "walk" or pull up on the footing, it is advisable to make the hole a little wider at the bottom.

Ready-mixed concrete

Concrete is made by mixing water with gravel and portland cement. For small jobs, such as footings, you can buy bags of ready-mixed concrete that contain gravel and portland cement in the proper proportion. Add water according to the directions on the bag.

Ready-mixed comes in 60-pound and 90-pound bags. A 60-pound bag of ready-mixed equals half a cubic foot of concrete. This is enough for one footing if you are in a frost-free area or the frost line is less than 2 feet deep. A 90-pound bag is enough for one footing up to 36 inches deep.

To extend the life of the post, the concrete must never completely encase bottom of post. After putting post into hole, throw in a few handfuls of dirt before pouring in concrete. This allows moisture that accumulates in the wood to drain into the ground.

An alternative

If the project is not permanent—that is, if it will be removed in six months or a year—using concrete is not mandatory. Just tamp dirt into hole around post a little at a time, layer by layer, with the handle of a shovel. This makes an adequate anchor.

Nailing a couple of crosspieces of scrap 1-by to the bottom of the post helps secure it a little better from upward pressure if you do not use concrete.

Two styles of post anchors

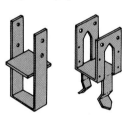

Post-anchor footing

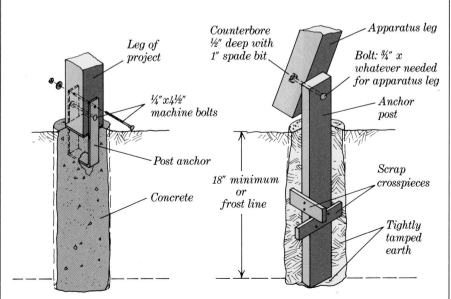

Leg of project

¼"x4½" machine bolts

Post anchor

Concrete

Alternate footing

Counterbore ½" deep with 1" spade bit

Apparatus leg

Bolt: ¾" x whatever needed for apparatus leg

Anchor post

18" minimum or frost line

Scrap crosspieces

Tightly tamped earth

Construction guidelines

Each of the four play structures in the following chapter was built to present a unique appearance and illustrate a different construction technique. The idea was to create a "cookbook" with specific "recipes" that you could follow with predictable results. It is possible to mix and match ideas from the various projects to customize your structure. For example, you may wish to save some money by using common plywood instead of the imported 9-ply specified for the Fitness Gym. Generally such substitutions can be made freely; however, structural elements such as swing beams should not be an area of economizing. Parts subject to rot and decay are other examples where you may wish to use materials that differ from the specifications in the materials lists.

Protecting wood from decay

Play structures made from wood are visually appealing and can be fun to build. But wood presents some problems. A play structure, like yard furniture, differs from a house because it has no outside skin to seal out moisture. Dirt and water will get into all the nooks and crannies of the structure, and this is where rot and insects will invade. Painting, especially with a penetrating wood preservative that is safe for contact, will help. All heart redwood naturally resists decay but can be expensive. It is also relatively soft and weak, so it should not be used for swing beams unless it is twice as thick as the Douglas fir beam used for the same application.

Pressure-treated wood

Pressure-treated wood is stronger and better protected from rot than redwood. Standard lumber such as Douglas fir or hemlock, when protected with wood preservative applied during construction, will not last as long as pressure-treated lumber.

Pressure-treated lumber is slightly green or beige in color and does not darken if left to weather. When buying it, specify whether it is for ground contact (LP-22) or above ground (LP-2) use. Sometimes it is incised or punctured on the surface to facilitate penetration of chemicals. For projects where a smooth, unblemished appearance is important, ask for pressure-treated lumber that has not been incised. It is also worth the extra cost to buy lumber that is kiln-dried after treatment (KDAT) to avoid extensive warping.

If you expect to use the structure for only a few years and then remove it, untreated wood will work. Otherwise, you need to protect the wood. Since rotting occurs mainly where wood touches ground, consider applying wood preservative only to these locations. Ask the lumberyard dealer to help select the best option for your local conditions and durability requirements.

If you choose to apply wood preservative yourself, your success in protecting wood from rot and insects depends on the chemicals you apply. These have varying degrees of toxicity. The material most commonly recommended by professionals is chromated copper arsenate (CCA). CCA has been reviewed by both the Environmental Protection Agency (EPA) and the Federal Food and Drug Administration and has been found acceptable when used according to directions.

Manufacturers of pressure-treated lumber issue a Consumer Information Sheet wherever the lumber is sold. This sheet contains safety tips for working with pressure-treated wood. The EPA guidelines suggest:
☐ Wear goggles and dust mask
☐ Perform work outdoors
☐ Dispose of treated wood by ordinary trash collection or burial
☐ Do not burn treated wood in open fires or indoor stoves or fireplaces
☐ After working with the wood and before eating, drinking, and use of tobacco products, thoroughly wash exposed areas
☐ Launder clothes before reuse; wash clothes separately

Costs

Choice of materials, whether for appearance or durability, will affect the final cost of the play structure. Redwood construction will cost more than standard lumber. The four projects made in this book were built for just under $400 each. This price will vary depending on the materials used.

Construction

Ease of construction will depend on whether you are more of a carpenter or a cabinetmaker. The Split-level Playhouse and A-frame Clubhouse are well suited for the carpenter who has the equipment and experience to handle the large 4-by structural components. On the other hand, the Creative Climber and Fitness Gym use more lightweight materials but require greater accuracy and would appeal to those who prefer a cabinet shop-type of approach.

The designs in this book provide two kinds of portability: moving from place to place within the yard and disassembling the unit for shipment to a new home. The A-frame Clubhouse unit itself is heavy, but can be taken apart for shipment. The Fitness Gym and Creative Climber are also movable. Both knock down into components that are easy to ship. The Split-level Playhouse is the most difficult to take apart and move.

Using the right tool for the job is the key to safe and simple assembly when you build play equipment. Rent or borrow tools called for in the project instructions if you do not own them. Construction will be much faster if you do.

Tools

The step-by-step instructions call for the use of tools such as routers and large drills that you may not own. Generally, these tools can be rented for a nominal charge and will make construction more enjoyable, accurate, and safe.

For the most part, nails have been avoided except in the Split-level Playhouse, which calls for standard carpentry construction techniques. Nails, when used on outdoor play structures, tend to back out and rise after a year or two. Instead of nails, the specifications call for galvanized multipurpose screws. This newly developed fastening device initially served to attach drywall to sheet-metal studs. The screws can be found in hardware stores and large lumber stores under a variety of names: galvanized drywall screws, "zip" screws, galvanized exterior screws, or bugle-head exterior screws.

These screws work in many different materials. They are thin and have an aggressive thread and a sharp point—qualities that allow them to be driven easily without a predrilled hole. Generally, they are used in combination with a battery-powered screwdriver. These, too, may be rented but they are also inexpensive to purchase. Using galvanized multipurpose screws instead of nails means that structures are easier to disassemble if the need should arise.

Where nails are specified, it is recommended that you use galvanized nails since they resist rusting in outdoor use.

Site locations and storage

Selecting the proper location for a play space may be one of the most important factors to the success of a project. You may have little choice about where to place a play structure. But if you do, several factors should be considered:

Supervision

You will be able to properly supervise your children if you can easily monitor their play from several key points within house: kitchen window, back door, or deck.

Appearance

Neighbors may object to a play structure that overlooks their backyard, especially if they do not have children themselves. Unless handled with care, your play structure could be the source of persistent problems. Consult your neighbors if the equipment will be visible from their homes. If local zoning permits, install a higher-than-normal fence on a section of your lot line.

Drainage

What happens to the water when it rains? If you have problems with standing water during wet seasons, install a drainage system. Generally a shallow trench with drain tile and gravel will be effective. If the problem is more extensive, consider consulting a landscape contractor for other solutions.

Storage

A place for toy storage should be planned as a component of the play area. Loose parts last longer if protected. Good storage also enhances children's play: It removes the clutter of toys that are not used for the current activity. Simple low shelving is best because children can see and retrieve toys. Wooden boxes do not work as well because the items at the bottom are often overlooked. Plastic milk-bottle crates make excellent storage. Not only do they provide stacked storage but they can also be used as construction elements in children's play. Whatever material or design is chosen, place storage as close to the play area as possible.

PLAY PROJECTS

I f you haven't already done so, read the introduction to this book on pages 5–17. It describes ways that play structures help children grow. Your children's delight in play keeps them active, inventive, and healthy. Complex and creative play structures, such as those described and illustrated on the following pages, provide for a variety of activities and foster imaginative play.

   The projects in this chapter represent four basic play structures. One design is not "better" than another. Each offers a distinctive mix of features, appearance, ease of construction, and portability. Some designs are based on classic concepts; others represent new approaches unique to this book. Choose one that appeals to you and your children, that you can afford, and that suits your building talents.

   Illustrations at the end of each project show the space required for the different pieces of play equipment. Be sure to check these and plan accordingly; the projects are quite large when all the options are included.

Selecting a design and building a play structure yourself not only saves money, but also allows you to match the features of the equipment to your child's personal preferences and physical abilities.

A-FRAME CLUBHOUSE

The A-frame is the most familiar shape for backyard play equipment. Its geometry makes construction simple and efficient, and its framework is naturally rigid. The structure rests on the ground without footed posts, although footings are recommended (see page 34).

Construction is fairly easy, but you will need tools large enough to handle 4-inch-thick wood and the skill to cut angles.

Any type of slide can be attached, but the one shown here—a banister slide using standard pipe fittings—is the simplest. The lower section of the A-frame is bordered with 8-inch redwood so this area can be filled with sand. You can build a ring trek extension using a longer main beam, or add it as a second phase. Later installation requires a splice where the new ring beam joins the swing beam.

The tent can be made without sewing if you use rip-stop nylon. The fabric is held with strips of wood nailed in place.

For this structure, redwood was used for the frame, but fir is used for the swing beam for extra strength. To ensure that the wood you choose is long-lasting, see "Protecting wood from decay" on page 35.

The A-frame Clubhouse is both hide-out and climbing structure. Adding the banister slide, fire pole, and swing beam increases the opportunity for physical challenge.

A-frame Clubhouse

Materials list

Main clubhouse structure

4x4
4 pieces 102" long for legs

2x8
2 pieces 55" long for sides of base
2 pieces 107" long for
    front and back of base

2x4
2 pieces 86" long for climbing rungs
2 pieces 70½" long for climbing rungs
2 pieces 12" long for beam braces
    (cut from rung scrap)
2 pieces 55" long for deck supports
3 pieces 93" long for deck joists
2 pieces 48" long for deck edges

½" ACX plywood
2 pieces 48"x45" for
    front and back wall panels

⅝" ACX plywood
1 piece 4x8 for flooring

2x8
2 pieces 43" long for shelves

1x8
2 pieces 32" long for shelf sides

Hardware and miscellaneous
12 carriage bolts ⅜"x2½"; nuts, washers
32 carriage bolts ⅜"x5"; nuts, washers
2 carriage bolts ½"x8"; nuts, washers
4 sheet-metal right-angle braces 3"
36 galvanized multipurpose
    screws 1¼"x#6
24 galvanized multipurpose
    screws 1¾"x#6
¼ lb HDG box nails 16d
Ready-mixed concrete: See "Footings" on
    pages 34–35 for amount needed

Swing beam

4x6 select structural fir
1 piece 14' long for beam

4x4
2 pieces 102" long for end support

2x4
1 piece 108" long for end support base
1 piece 12" long for beam brace

Hardware and miscellaneous
4 carriage bolts ⅜"x5"; nuts, washers
1 carriage bolt ½"x8"; nut, washer
Ready-mixed concrete: See "Footings" on
    pages 34–35 for amount needed

Tent

2x4
4 pieces 96" long for frame legs
1 piece 51" long for frame ridge
2 pieces 48" long for horizontal
    frame braces

Scrap plywood
4 triangular gussets cut
    from two 8" squares

1x2 redwood lath
10 pieces 48" long for top tack strips
2 pieces 72" long for diagonal braces
4 pieces 96" long for side tack strips

Hardware and miscellaneous
1 piece rip-stop nylon fabric
    54"x5½ yd long for tent top
4 carriage bolts ⅜"x3"; nuts, washers
2 carriage bolts ¼"x4"; nuts, washers
20 galvanized multipurpose
    screws 1"x#6
4 galvanized multipurpose
    screws 2"x#6
8 galvanized multipurpose
    screws 3¾"x#6
¼ lb HDG box nails 6d
Staple gun or tacks

Fire pole

Hardware and miscellaneous
1 piece of 1" dia galvanized iron pipe
    100" long (one end threaded)
1 floor flange 1" dia
4 flat-head wood screws 1½"x#10

Banister slide

Hardware and miscellaneous
3 pieces of 1" dia galvanized iron pipe
    126" long (one end threaded)
2 pipe nipples 1"dia x 8"
2 pipe nipples 1"dia x 5"
3 tees 1" dia
2 street elbows 1" dia
2 floor flanges 1" dia
8 flat-head machine bolts ¼"x1";
    nuts, washers

Optional ring trek

4x6
1 piece 24' long (instead of swing beam)
    or 1 piece 12' long spliced
    to swing beam

4x4
2 pieces 102" long for end support legs

2x4
1 piece 108" long for end support base

Hardware and miscellaneous
4 carriage bolts ⅜"x5"; nuts, washers
1 carriage bolt ½"x8"; nut, washer
3 carriage bolts ½"x6"; nuts, washers
2 carriage bolts ½"x6"; nuts, washers
    if beam is spliced
5 pieces of ⅜" dia rope
    24" long for hand rings
5 pieces of 1" (or more) dia dowel
    8" long for hand rings

Tools needed

Carpenter's square and level (or combination square); 25' tape measure; handsaw or circular saw; saber saw; wood rasp
or coarse sandpaper; electric drill; hammer; screwdriver (electric preferred with
#2 Phillips bit); flatblade screwdriver;
protractor and sliding bevel; 9/16" and ¾"
ratchet and sockets; ⅜" and ½" drill bits;
1" and 1⅜" spade bits

A-frame Clubhouse

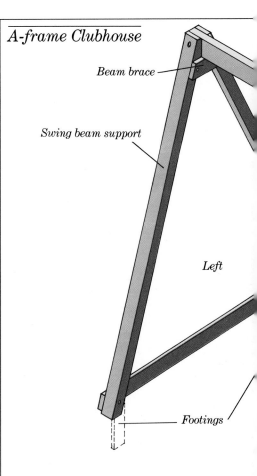

Beam brace

Swing beam support

Left

Footings

Front

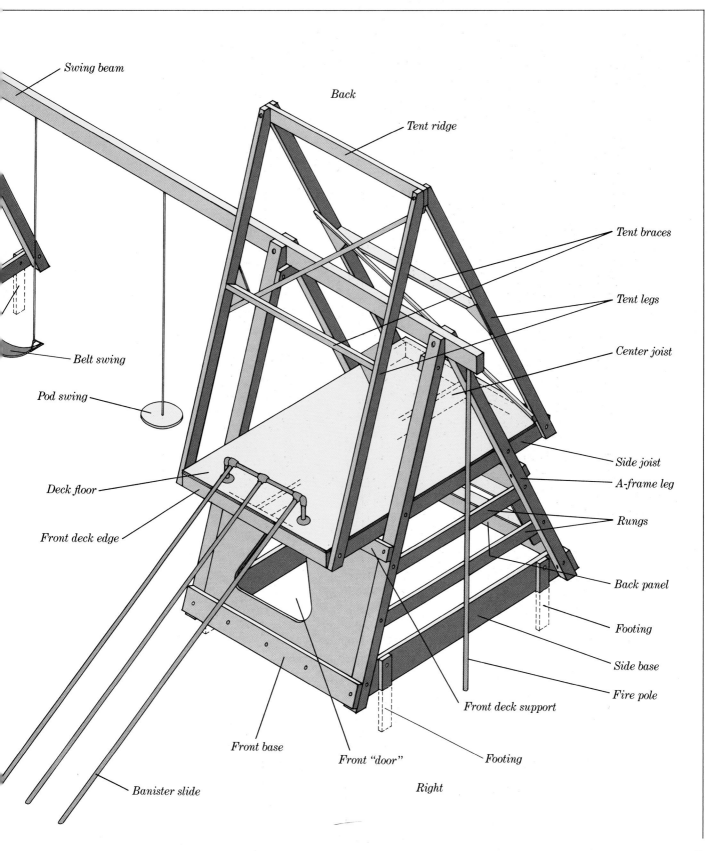

Swing beam

Back

Tent ridge

Tent braces

Tent legs

Belt swing

Center joist

Pod swing

Side joist

A-frame leg

Deck floor

Rungs

Front deck edge

Back panel

Footing

Side base

Fire pole

Front deck support

Front base

Front "door"

Footing

Banister slide

Right

A-frame Clubhouse

Build the A-frames

Two identical A-frame assemblies form the sides of the clubhouse. When cutting the pieces, note that the geometry is basically an equilateral triangle, and that the angle-cuts are all 60 degrees, with the exception of the 30-degree cuts at the top, which form the notch for the top cross beam (see Figures A-1 and A-2). Cut rungs and baseboards ½ inch short on each end to allow for front and back plywood panels.

Assemble A-frames using ⅜-inch by 5-inch bolt connections shown in Figure A-3. Complete each outer triangle first, including its beam brace, then bolt on rungs and side joists (Figures A-4 and A-5).

The clubhouse frame

Prepare clubhouse site by leveling an area approximately 5 feet by 10 feet. Cut the two side-base pieces and two deck supports to 55 inches each. With an assistant, carry A-frames and crosspieces to the site. Stand A-frames up (make sure that rungs and side joists are on the "inner" sides), and clamp the 55-inch base and support pieces in place. Drill, counterbore, and bolt all the connections using twelve ⅜-inch by 5-inch carriage bolts (Figures B-1 and B-2).

Cut the front and back panels from ½-inch plywood. Each panel is 48 inches wide by 45 inches high. Save the back panel for later, but cut a triangular door in the front panel, as follows: Scribe a line 8 inches up from the bottom edge of the panel. Mark the left and right "corners" of the triangle on the baseline, 2 inches in from the panel sides. The top "corner" is located at the midpoint of the panel, 2 inches down from the top edge. Connect the three "corners" to form a triangle, then use a 12-inch-diameter object (such as a 5-gallon paint can, or a large kitchen pot or pan) to scribe an arc inside each corner. Cut the rounded triangular opening with a saber saw.

Figure A-1   A-frame assembly

Position side joist so that overhang (a) is equal on each end

See Figure A-4 for notch detail

See Figure A-3 for all connections

Side joist

½" space for plywood panels

Rungs

Baseboard

48"

34½"

21"

107"

Figure A-2   A-frame legs

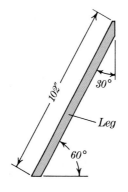

102"

30°

Leg

60°

Figure A-3   Typical A-frame bolt connection

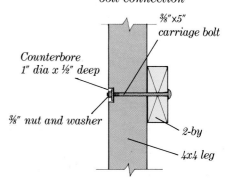

⅜"×5" carriage bolt

Counterbore 1" dia x ½" deep

⅜" nut and washer

2-by

4x4 leg

Figure A-4   Tops of A-frames

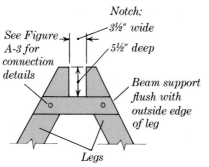

Notch: 3½" wide 5½" deep

See Figure A-3 for connection details

Beam support flush with outside edge of leg

Legs

Figure A-5   Bottoms of A-frames

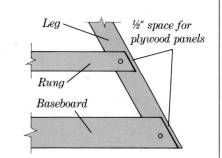

Leg

½" space for plywood panels

Rung

Baseboard

Apply finish to the panel now, before mounting. To mount panel, loosen base-board bolts and slide in the panel (see Figure C). Clamp top of panel to deck support, then drill and bolt it in position, using ³⁄₈-inch by 2¹⁄₂-inch carriage bolts.

Add the deck

Using 16 penny (d) nails, facenail 48-inch deck edges to the ends of the front and back side joist extensions. Reinforce the four inside corners by attaching 3-inch right-angle brackets with 1¹⁄₄-inch by No. 6 galvanized multipurpose screws. Facenail a 93-inch center joist between front and rear cross joists. Lay a 48-inch by 96-inch sheet of plywood onto joists, smooth side up. Drive twenty-four 1³⁄₄-inch by No. 6 galvanized multipurpose screws through plywood into joists.

If you are not adding the swing beam (shown on next page), mount a 96-inch 4 by 6 in the notches at the top of the A-frames. Allow an equal overhang at each end, and secure it using the method described for the swing beam on the next page.

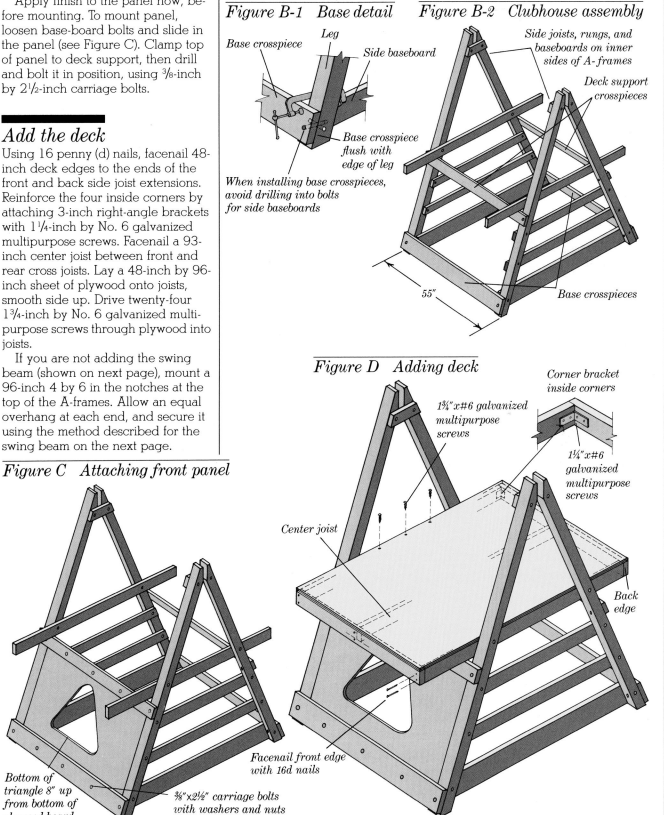

Figure B-1   Base detail

Base crosspiece
Leg
Side baseboard
Base crosspiece flush with edge of leg
When installing base crosspieces, avoid drilling into bolts for side baseboards

Figure B-2   Clubhouse assembly

Side joists, rungs, and baseboards on inner sides of A-frames
Deck support crosspieces
55"
Base crosspieces

Figure D   Adding deck

1³⁄₄"x#6 galvanized multipurpose screws
Corner bracket inside corners
1¹⁄₄"x#6 galvanized multipurpose screws
Center joist
Back edge
Facenail front edge with 16d nails

Figure C   Attaching front panel

Bottom of triangle 8" up from bottom of plywood board
³⁄₈"x2¹⁄₂" carriage bolts with washers and nuts

A-frame Clubhouse

Add the swing beam

Using angles of 60 degrees and 30 degrees, measure and cut the material for the A-shaped swing-beam end-support assembly much as you did for the A-frame Clubhouse sides. Figures E and E-1 illustrate the details of the swing-beam end support.

Install the swing beam

Select a true and structurally sound 4 by 6 for the swing beam. With an assistant or two, slide beam up into notches atop A-frame Clubhouse. Note that beam overhangs 20 inches at right end. Support the outer end of the beam temporarily while you counterbore, drill, and bolt the beam to the top of the clubhouse using ½-inch by 8-inch carriage bolts (set parallel to the ground). Figure E-1 shows details of these fittings.

Level the ground or add fill, if necessary, as you locate the swing-beam end support at the outer end of the swing beam. After you adjust it to the right height—with the beam solidly in notch, and the end-support frame plumb and parallel to clubhouse—counterbore, drill, and bolt beam into end-support notch using a ½-inch by 8-inch carriage bolt.

To stabilize the swing-beam end support, attach add-on footings (see page 34). An additional pair of footings is also recommended at the right side of the clubhouse.

On page 23 you will find an assortment of swings and trapeze bars that you can buy or make and attach to the swing beam.

To use these components with the swing beam, follow the instructions that accompany the selected items.

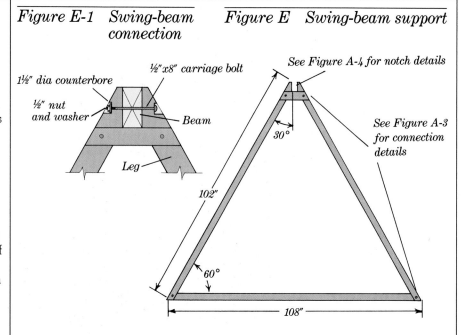

Figure E-1 Swing-beam connection

1½" dia counterbore
½" nut and washer
½"x8" carriage bolt
Beam
Leg

Figure E Swing-beam support

See Figure A-4 for notch details
See Figure A-3 for connection details
30°
102"
60°
108"

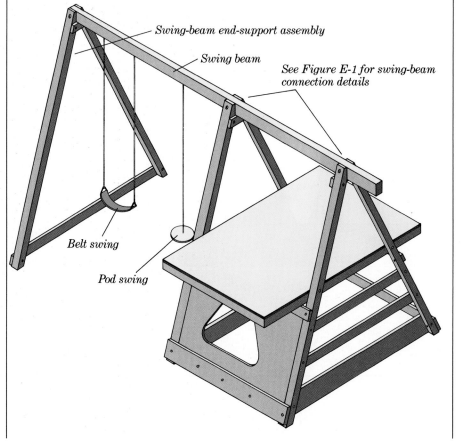

Figure F Swing-beam installation

Swing-beam end-support assembly
Swing beam
See Figure E-1 for swing-beam connection details
Belt swing
Pod swing

Build the tent frame

Incorporating angles of 60 degrees and 30 degrees, cut the four tent legs from 2 by 4s (Figure G-1). Also from 2 by 4s, cut the 51-inch frame ridge and two 48-inch tent frame braces. Clamp legs to deck side joists. Drill ³⁄₈-inch holes, and attach legs with ³⁄₈-inch by 3-inch carriage bolts. With a helper, hold legs in place and set ridge. Drill 1-inch counterbores and ¹⁄₄-inch holes (see Figure G-2), then fit ¹⁄₄-inch by 4-inch carriage bolts at each ridge-leg connection.

Using four 3³⁄₄-inch galvanized multipurpose screws, attach two horizontal braces. Cut four triangular gussets from two 8-inch squares of plywood (use scrap from triangular opening), and affix one gusset to each leg-brace joint with five 1-inch galvanized multipurpose screws. For stability, cut one diagonal brace per side from 1 by 2 stock, and attach one brace to upper inside of front side framing and other to lower inside of back side framing (see Figure G-1). Secure each brace with two 2-inch galvanized multipurpose screws.

Attach the tent

Cut a piece of fabric 54 inches wide and 152 inches long. Fold back and side edges in by 1¹⁄₂ inches and staple or tack fabric to tent frame, leaving area below front cross-brace open for banister slide. With remaining fabric, cover the tent sides (see photograph, page 40). Then nail 1 by 2s to the frame, covering the fabric edges (Figure H-1).

Add the fire pole

Dig an 18-inch hole under the swing beam extension, 16 inches to the right of the clubhouse side (Figure H-1). Thread the 100-inch fire-pole pipe into the floor flange, place bottom end of fire pole into hole in ground, and screw flange to bottom of swing beam extension using four 1¹⁄₂-inch by No. 10 flat-head wood screws (Figure H-2).

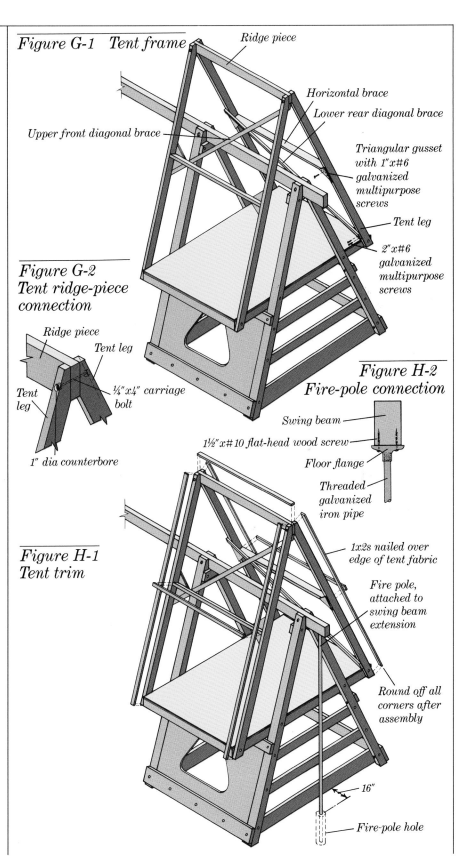

Figure G-1 Tent frame

Ridge piece

Horizontal brace

Lower rear diagonal brace

Upper front diagonal brace

Triangular gusset with 1"x#6 galvanized multipurpose screws

Tent leg

2"x#6 galvanized multipurpose screws

*Figure G-2
Tent ridge-piece connection*

Ridge piece

Tent leg

Tent leg

¹⁄₄"x4" carriage bolt

1" dia counterbore

*Figure H-2
Fire-pole connection*

Swing beam

1¹⁄₂"x#10 flat-head wood screw

Floor flange

Threaded galvanized iron pipe

*Figure H-1
Tent trim*

1x2s nailed over edge of tent fabric

Fire pole, attached to swing beam extension

Round off all corners after assembly

16"

Fire-pole hole

A-frame Clubhouse

Make a banister slide

Assemble nipples, elbows, tees, flanges, and pipes (Figure I). Position slide assembly on clubhouse. On the ground, mark the location of the slide pipe ends. Set slide assembly aside, and dig a trench 32 inches wide and 12 inches deep, tapering up toward clubhouse. Place slide into position, drill deck, and fit the 8 flat-head bolts, screwing on the nuts from the bottom. Backfill the trench. For other slide options, see pages 24–27.

Build the store panel

Locate the back panel that was set aside earlier. Cut a window 30 inches wide by 16 inches high, located 18 inches from the bottom, and centered from side to side.

Cut the two 2 by 8 shelves to 43 inches, and bevel-rip one edge of each to 30 degrees. With a helper, screw shelves to panel flush with top and bottom window openings and centered (2½ inches in from each side). Screw beveled edges to panel so shelves will be level when panel is in place (see Figure J). Use 1¼-inch by No. 6 galvanized multipurpose screws spaced every six inches.

To make the two shelf sides, cut a 30-degree angle on one end of each board. Then measure 32 inches from one corner, and make a parallel cut. Screw sides to ends of shelves and to panel using 1¼-inch by No. 6 galvanized multipurpose screws spaced every six inches. Position sides as you like, making sure that boards will clear deck support above shelves.

As an alternative to this design, you can set two loose shelves on the rungs of the A-frame. Use the shelves to mark the position of the cutout in the back panel, as it will be shorter and lower than the one in Figure J.

Paint panel and shelves now if they will be different from the clubhouse frame. Remove back baseboard temporarily to install back panel. Bolt panel in place as you did front panel (refer to Figure C, page 45).

Figure I   Banister slide

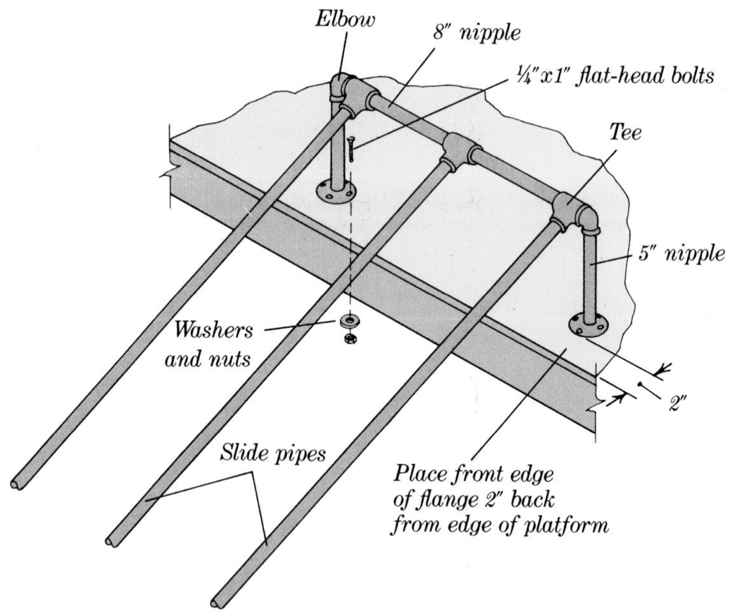

Elbow
8" nipple
¼"x1" flat-head bolts
Tee
5" nipple
Washers and nuts
2"
Slide pipes
Place front edge of flange 2" back from edge of platform

Figure J   Store panel (inside view)

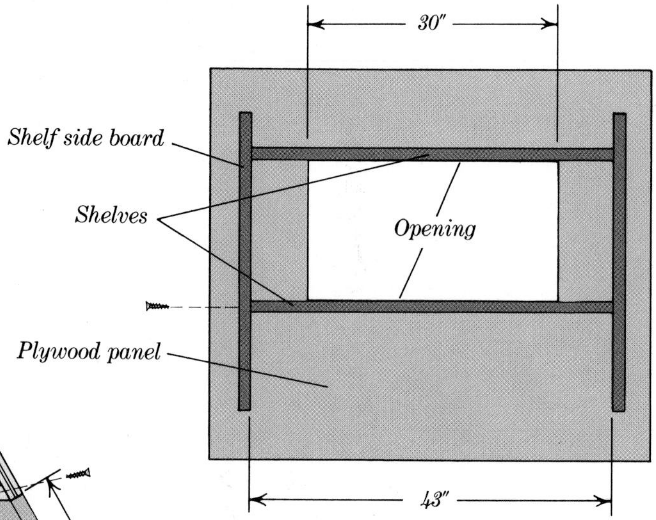

30"
Shelf side board
Shelves
Opening
Plywood panel
43"

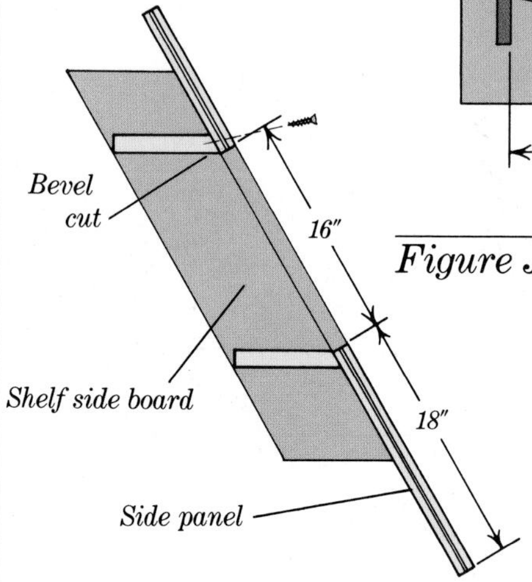

Figure J-1   Store panel (side view)

Bevel cut
16"
Shelf side board
Side panel
18"

Optional ring trek

To include the ring trek, you can use a longer beam or splice a 12-foot beam to the end of the existing swing beam. Do this by making a 16-inch-long half-lap joint and bolting it together with three ¹⁄₂-inch by 6-inch carriage bolts. Insert bolts from the bottom so that nuts and washers are on top of beam. Build an additional A-frame, following the instructions for the swing-beam end support (Figure E, page 46).

Drill beam for rings, as illustrated in Figure K-2. Make rings from 2-foot lengths of rope and 8-inch lengths of 1-inch (or more) wooden dowel, drilled 1¹⁄₂ inches in from each end to accept rope. To install rings, knot rope on either side of beam, pass rope through handles, and knot ends.

Maintenance

Tighten all fittings after three months, and check for worn or damaged parts. Repair or replace as necessary. Repeat this safety check six months later and once per year thereafter.

Figure K-1 Ring detail

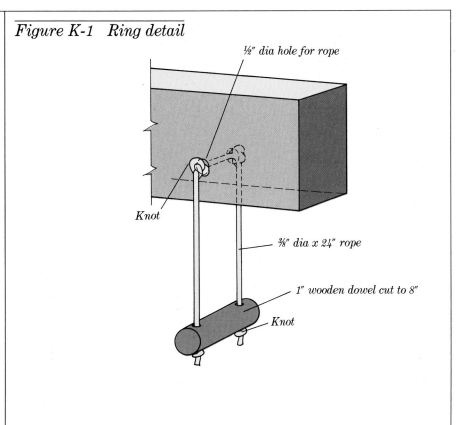

½" dia hole for rope

Knot

⅜" dia x 24" rope

1" wooden dowel cut to 8"

Knot

Figure K-2 Add ring trek

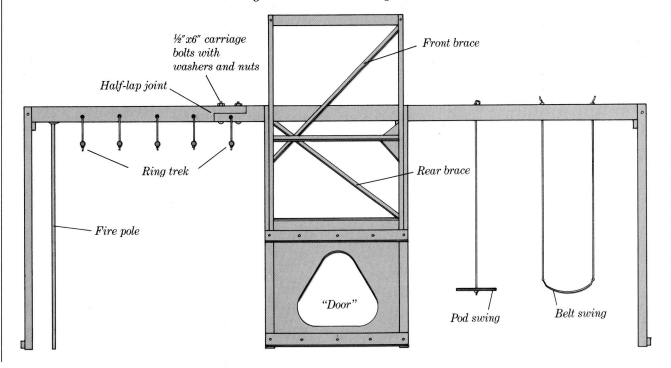

½"x6" carriage bolts with washers and nuts

Half-lap joint

Front brace

Rear brace

Ring trek

Fire pole

"Door"

Pod swing

Belt swing

A-frame Clubhouse

Space requirements

The A-frame Clubhouse may be assembled in different configurations or in phases. The illustrations on these pages show the actual size of the structures and the approximate total area required, including play safety zone as indicated by the loop drawn around each configuration. The smallest design is for the A-frame Clubhouse only. The medium-sized drawing includes the swing, and the largest design includes the ring trek.

A-frame Clubhouse

Clubhouse only (Use an 8-foot beam for the clubhouse only)

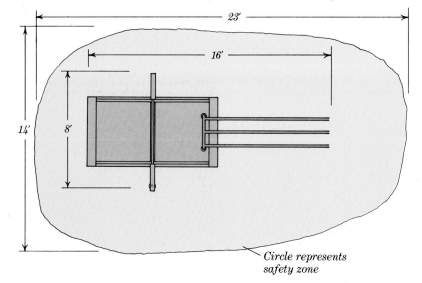

Circle represents safety zone

Clubhouse with swing extension

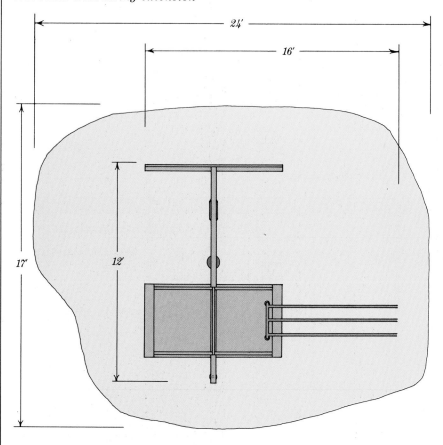

Clubhouse with both swing extension and ring trek

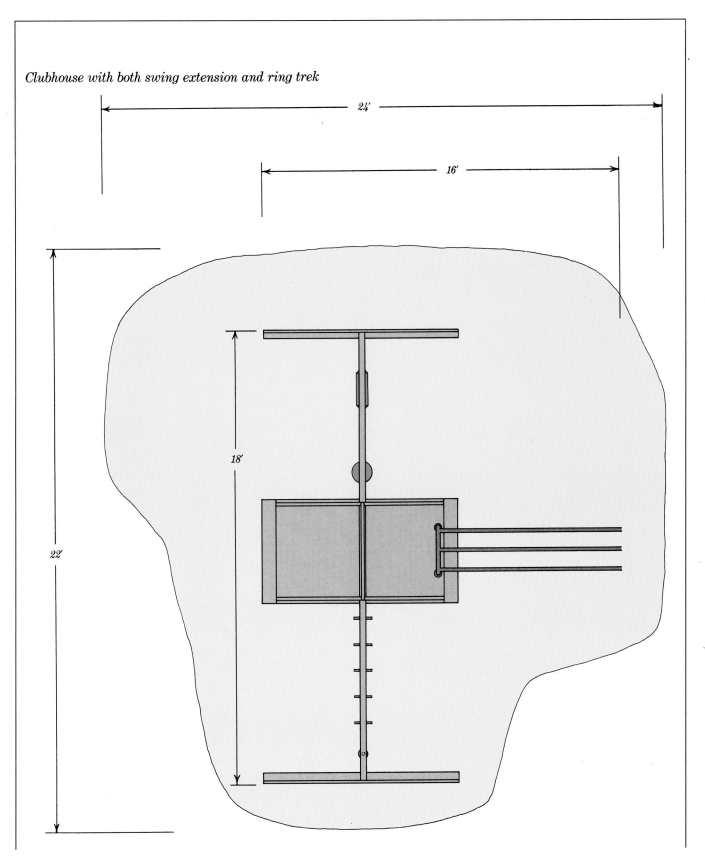

FITNESS GYM

T *he Fitness Gym is a structure with myriad uses. At the center is a play structure designed to capture the imagination of children. The tent-enclosed section has a door, windows, movable planks, an optional slide, and a fire pole. A beam extending from one side can be equipped with a variety of swings, the trapeze bar, or rings.*

The system of posts, rails, and rungs extending from the other side of the play structure is designed to serve both kids and grownups. This outstanding feature encourages simultaneous participation by adults and children—allowing recreational time together and giving adults an opportunity to set an example for fitness.

The Fitness Gym as shown in the photographs is constructed of select kiln-dried hemlock 2-bys, with imported 9-ply plywood used for the panels. A finish of clear varnish enhances the inherent beauty of the wood. The projects in this book display a variety of materials and finishes, so feel free to select a combination that appeals to you. To ensure that the wood you choose is durable, see ''Protecting wood from decay'' on page 35.

Although designed to optimize the exercise components of the structure, the Fitness Gym is, in every way, a place to play.

Fitness Gym

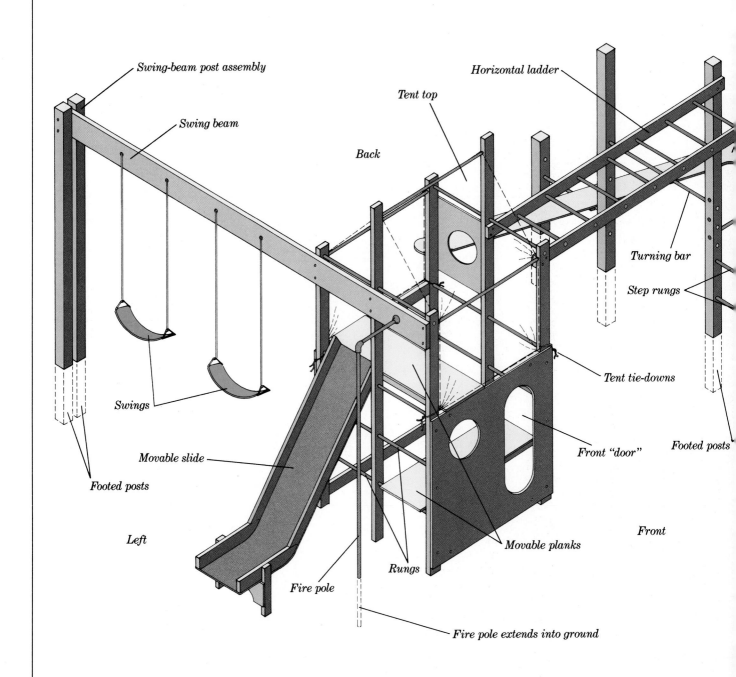

Fitness Gym

Swing-beam post assembly

Swing beam

Tent top

Back

Horizontal ladder

Turning bar

Step rungs

Swings

Tent tie-downs

Movable slide

Footed posts

Footed posts

Front "door"

Front

Left

Movable planks

Rungs

Fire pole

Fire pole extends into ground

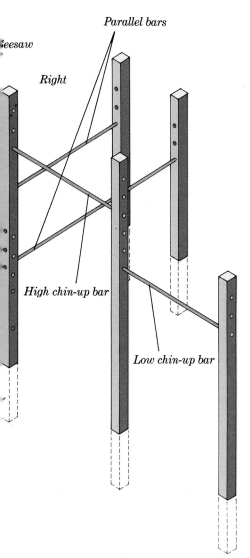

Seesaw

Right

Parallel bars

High chin-up bar

Low chin-up bar

Materials list

Subframes

2x4 fir
4 pieces 86″ long for posts
2 pieces 110″ long for posts

1″ dia hardwood dowel
8 pieces 46½″ long for subframe rungs

Hardware and miscellaneous
24 galvanized multipurpose
   screws 2″x#6

Structure assembly

½″ ACX plywood
2 pieces 48″x48″ for lower panels
1 piece 24″x24″ for upper panel
3 pieces 16″x48″ for planks

2x4 fir
4 pieces 41″ long for
   lower panel supports

2x2 fir
6 pieces 43½″ long for plank rails

**¾″ dia schedule 40 galvanized
  iron pipe, unthreaded**
3 pieces 47½″ long for upper cross rungs

Hardware and miscellaneous
20 carriage bolts ¼″x2″; washers, nuts
6 carriage bolts ¼″x1¾″;
   washers, cap nuts
4 carriage bolts ¼″x4″; washers, nuts
54 multipurpose
   galvanized screws 1½″x#6
6 oz bottle waterproof glue
Ready-mixed concrete: See ''Footings''
   on pages 34–35 for amount needed

Horizontal ladder

2x4 fir
2 pieces 96″ long for ladder rails

1″ dia hardwood dowel
7 pieces 21″ long for ladder rungs

Hardware and miscellaneous
14 galvanized multipurpose
   screws 2″x#6
4 carriage bolts ¼″x3″; nuts, washers
4 carriage bolts ¼″x5″; nuts, washers

Fitness array

4x4 fir
1 piece 48″ long for post
2 pieces 72″ long for posts
2 pieces 90″ long for posts
3 pieces 108″ long for posts

1″ dia hardwood dowel
2 pieces 28″ long for lower rungs

**¾″ dia schedule 40 galvanized
  iron pipe, unthreaded**
1 piece 36″ long for seesaw support
3 pieces 48″ long for fitness rungs
2 pieces 72″ long for parallel bars

Hardware and miscellaneous
4 galvanized multipurpose screws 2″x#6
12 carriage bolts ¼″x3½″;
   washers, wing nuts
Ready-mixed concrete: See ''Footings''
   on pages 34–35 for amount needed
1 qt wood preservative

Seesaw

2x10 vertical grain fir
1 piece 120″ long for seesaw plank

1x2 fir or pine
2 pieces 8″ long for seesaw cleats

Hardware and miscellaneous
4 carriage bolts ¼″x2¾″;
   washers, cap nuts

Fabric top

Hardware and miscellaneous
1 piece 43″x130″ rip-stop nylon
   for tent top
1 spool nylon or polyester thread
4 flexible nylon cords ¼″dia x 60″
   for tent tie-downs

Tools needed
Carpenter's square and level (or combination square); 25′ tape measure; handsaw or circular saw; saber saw; wood rasp or coarse sandpaper; electric drill; screwdriver (electric preferred with #2 Phillips bit); 7/16″ ratchet and socket; ¼″ and 3/16″ drill bits; ¾″ and 1″spade bits

Swing beam

2x8 select structural fir or equivalent
1 piece 16′ long for swing beam

**4x4 fir, redwood, or
  pressure-treated wood**
2 pieces 114″ long for swing beam posts

2x4 fir
2 pieces 24″ long for post blocks

Hardware and miscellaneous
6 carriage bolts ¼″x5″; washers, nuts
6 machine bolts 3/8″x9″; washers, nuts
Ready-mixed concrete: See ''Footings''
   on pages 34–35 for amount needed

Fitness Gym

Construct the subframe

Begin construction of the Fitness Gym by cutting and drilling the two vertical subframe components for the central structure. Two 2 by 4s at 86 inches and one 2 by 4 at 110 inches, as well as four 1-inch dowels at 46½ inches each, are required for each subframe. Using the measurements shown in Figure A, drill the 2 by 4s to accept the dowels. Center 1-inch

bores on the faces of the boards. Finishing the last bit of each bore from the back of the board will reduce splintering.

Slide pieces together, taking care to place the tall post between the shorter end posts. Drill a ³⁄₃₂-inch pilot hole, and secure each post-to-rung connection with a 2-inch by No. 6 multipurpose screw (see Figure A-1). Take care to make the outer posts flush with the ends of the dowels.

Erect the central structure

The central structure includes subframes (as prepared at the left), metal cross rungs, and plywood panels. First, cut three pieces of ¾-inch schedule 40 unthreaded pipe to 47½ inches each. Cut the two 48-inch squares from ½-inch ACX plywood. Lay out and cut the openings in the plywood, as shown in Figure B. Attach two 41-inch 2 by 4 lower panel supports to the back of each panel with two 2-inch carriage bolts in each support. Counterbore the back of the 2 by 4 for the nuts and washers (see detail in Figure B).

Using a drill guide, bore six 1-inch holes in the subframe posts, 4 inches from the top of each 2 by 4, to accept upper cross rungs (Figure C-1). A drill guide will drill holes straight and also keep them centered on the edges of the 2 by 4s. Set the depth-stop on the drill guide so that bore is 3¼ inches deep—¼ inch short of passing through the 2 by 4 post.

Fit subframes, lower panel assemblies, and upper cross rungs together (Figure C) as follows: Drill and bolt panels to subframes, taking care to square them up first. Use three ¼-inch by 2-inch carriage bolts along each side of each lower panel. Remember to counterbore backs of these connections.

Carefully drill each pipe-to-post connection to accept a ¼-inch by 1¾-inch carriage bolt (Figure C-1). Cap nuts, instead of counterbores, are used on these connections.

Figure A   Constructing subframe

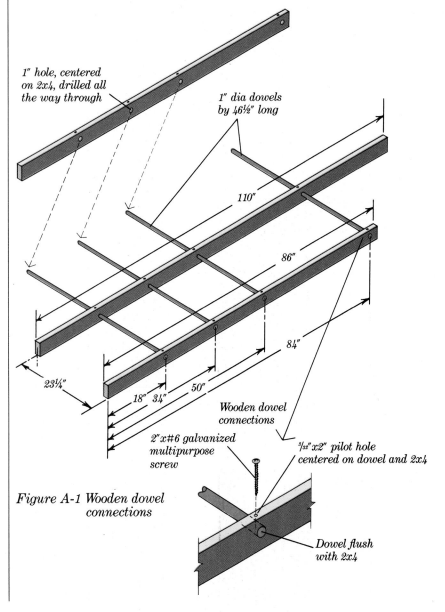

1" hole, centered on 2x4, drilled all the way through

1" dia dowels by 46½" long

110"

86"

84"

23¼"

18" 34" 50"

Wooden dowel connections

2"x#6 galvanized multipurpose screw

³⁄₃₂"x2" pilot hole centered on dowel and 2x4

Dowel flush with 2x4

Figure A-1 Wooden dowel connections

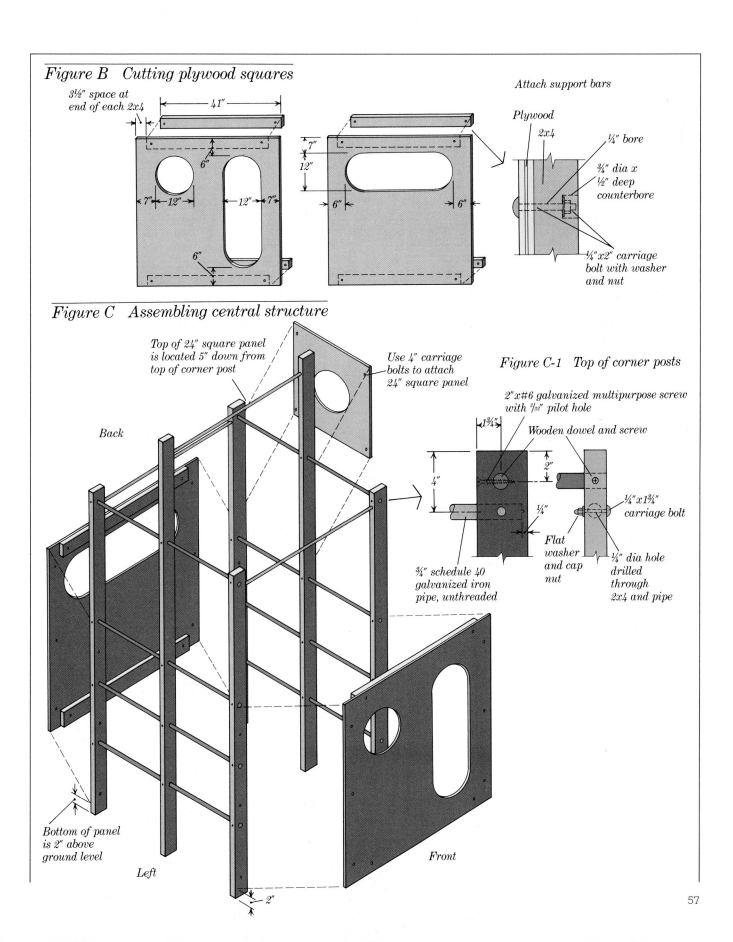

Figure B   Cutting plywood squares

3½" space at end of each 2x4

41"

7"
6"
7"   12"   12"   7"
6"

7"
12"
6"   6"

Attach support bars

Plywood
2x4
¼" bore
¾" dia x ½" deep counterbore
¼" x 2" carriage bolt with washer and nut

Figure C   Assembling central structure

Top of 24" square panel is located 5" down from top of corner post

Use 4" carriage bolts to attach 24" square panel

Back

Figure C-1   Top of corner posts

2" x #6 galvanized multipurpose screw with ³/₃₂" pilot hole

Wooden dowel and screw

1¾"
4"
2"
¼"

¾" schedule 40 galvanized iron pipe, unthreaded

Flat washer and cap nut

¼" x 1¾" carriage bolt

¼" dia hole drilled through 2x4 and pipe

Bottom of panel is 2" above ground level

Left

Front

2"

57

Fitness Gym

The Fitness Gym is light enough to be moved easily, once completed. To add stability in a given location, you will need two footings (see pages 34–35). Use add-on footings if your climate requires footings deeper than 18 inches. If you construct the exercise center on the right side, place footings at right-front and right-back corners. If you incorporate the swing beam, you will need footings at rear-left and rear-right corners. The central structure, if used alone, must be footed on opposing corners, and preferably on all four corners.

Finally, for added stability cut the 24-inch-square upper panel from 1/2-inch ACX plywood. Cut a 12-inch-diameter circle in the center, and attach the panel to the upper-right side of the central structure with four 1/2-inch by 4-inch carriage bolts. In the event you are *not* going to add the swing beam, cut and place a matching 24-inch-square on the upper part of the left side (either toward the front or toward the back will do).

Build movable planks

Cut the three 16-inch by 48-inch planks. Sand edges, and attach 2 by 2 plank rails to the bottom of each plank (Figure D). Use waterproof glue and 1 1/2-inch by No. 6 screws to affix rails, checking to make sure there is a 2 1/4-inch inset at each end. Round off corners of planks and rails. Prime and paint plank assemblies with a durable finish.

Add the fitness center

The fitness center consists of components designed to support a variety of activities for children and adults. Individual exercise stations, which can be placed along an exercise course, are shown in Chapter 1, pages 28–31.

The fitness center is attached to the central structure of the Fitness Gym by a horizontal ladder (Figure E). To make the ladder, cut seven 1-inch hardwood dowel rungs, each 21 inches long. In each of the two 96-inch rails, drill seven 1-inch holes, centered edge to edge, and spaced at 12-inch intervals on center. Complete these holes from the other side to avoid splintering. Assemble rungs and rails, making sure rails are flush with rung ends. Then drill a 3/32-inch pilot hole through the top of the rail, into each dowel. Use 2-inch by No. 6 galvanized multipurpose screws to secure the connections.

Build the fitness array

Note that in Figure E the orientation is from the *right* side of the structure illustrated on pages 54–55. The central structure should be attached to the end of the horizontal ladder. To build the array shown in Figure E, you will need eight posts: three at 108 inches, two at 90 inches, two at 72 inches, and one at 48 inches. Since the posts are set into concrete footings, the lower 24 inches of each must be treated with wood preservative. Alternatively, you can purchase pressure-treated posts or use rot-resistant redwood posts. (See "Protecting wood from decay," page 35.)

Once posts are cut to proper lengths, follow the dimensions shown in Figure E for drilling the holes for the movable bars. The holes are drilled completely through the posts and are slightly oversize (1 1/8 inches) to allow removal and replacement of rungs. Use a drill guide or drill press to ensure that holes are straight, and sand edges of each hole. The holes are positioned to provide a variety of bar and rung placements, and it is best to drill *all* the holes at this stage.

Figure D   Movable planks

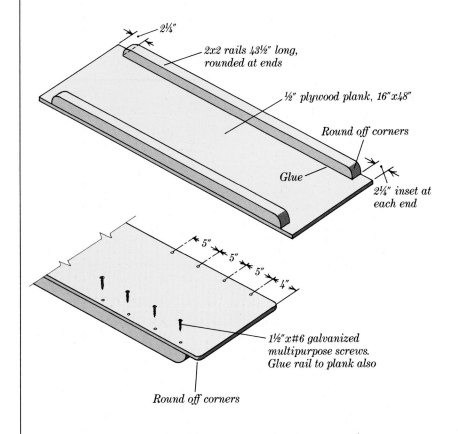

2 1/4"

2x2 rails 43 1/2" long, rounded at ends

1/2" plywood plank, 16"x48"

Round off corners

Glue

2 1/4" inset at each end

5" 5" 5" 4"

1 1/2"x#6 galvanized multipurpose screws. Glue rail to plank also

Round off corners

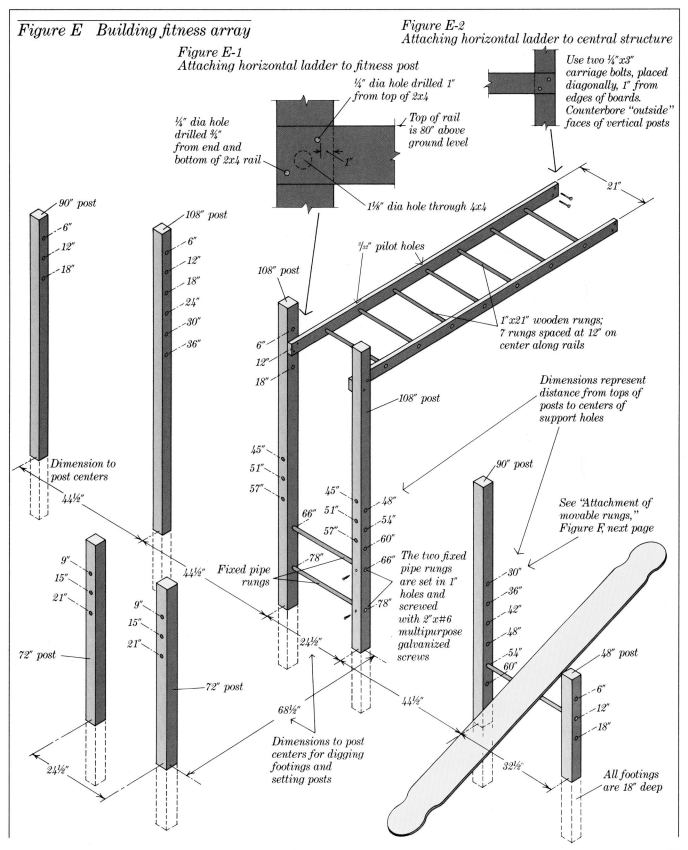

Figure E   Building fitness array

Figure E-1
Attaching horizontal ladder to fitness post

Figure E-2
Attaching horizontal ladder to central structure

¼" dia hole drilled 1" from top of 2x4

Use two ¼"x3" carriage bolts, placed diagonally, 1" from edges of boards. Counterbore "outside" faces of vertical posts

¼" dia hole drilled ¾" from end and bottom of 2x4 rail

Top of rail is 80" above ground level

1⅛" dia hole through 4x4

³/₃₂" pilot holes

21"

90" post
6"
12"
18"

108" post
6"
12"
18"
24"
30"
36"

108" post
6"
12"
18"

1"x21" wooden rungs; 7 rungs spaced at 12" on center along rails

108" post

Dimension to post centers

44½"

45"
51"
57"

45"
51"
57"

48"
54"
60"
66"

Dimensions represent distance from tops of posts to centers of support holes

90" post

30"
36"
42"
48"
54"
60"

See "Attachment of movable rungs," Figure F, next page

9"
15"
21"

9"
15"
21"

72" post

44½"

Fixed pipe rungs

66"
78"
78"

The two fixed pipe rungs are set in 1" holes and screwed with 2"x#6 multipurpose galvanized screws

48" post
6"
12"
18"

72" post

24½"

68½"

Dimensions to post centers for digging footings and setting posts

24½"

44½"

32½"

All footings are 18" deep

Fitness Gym

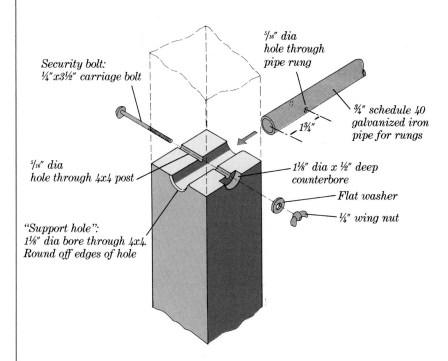

*Figure F   Attachment of movable rungs
(cross section through post)*

Security bolt:
¼"x3½" carriage bolt

⁵/₁₆" dia
hole through
pipe rung

¾" schedule 40
galvanized iron
pipe for rungs

1¾"

⁵/₁₆" dia
hole through 4x4 post

1⅛" dia x ½" deep
counterbore

Flat washer

¼" wing nut

"Support hole":
1⅛" dia bore through 4x4.
Round off edges of hole

The support holes for the movable rungs are 1⅛ inches in diameter, but note that the two lower rungs (below the end of the horizontal ladder) are fixed hardwood dowel rungs 28 inches long. These require a 1-inch hole and are secured with galvanized multipurpose screws. (For extra strength, the lower rungs can be made from metal pipe and attached in the same manner as the metal bars below.)

Each movable metal bar is held in its support holes by ¼-inch carriage bolts with wing nuts (for convenient removal and replacement). Predrill each metal bar with a ⁵/₁₆-inch-diameter hole centered 1¾ inches from each end. If possible, drill these, or have these drilled, on a drill press. The holes must be aligned parallel to each other. Sand or file holes to remove burrs or sharp edges. Drill the 4 by 4 posts with ⁵/₁₆-inch holes perpendicular to the support holes. These holes for the bolts must be

level with the center axis of the 1⅛-inch support holes, and they must be located 1¾ inches from the edges of the posts. See detail illustration, Figure F. Use a 1⅛-inch bit to make a counterbore at each bolt hole.

Set the posts

Digging footing holes and setting posts are critical steps in the construction of the fitness array. (Pages 34–35 have additional information on footings which you should read now if you haven't already.) As shown in Figure E, six of the eight posts share a common centerline. In this figure the centerline of the posts is a line 90¾ inches to the left of the central structure. Figure E shows how the posts are spaced along this line. The two posts at the end of the horizontal ladder act as the reference point for all the posts, since the horizontal ladder must extend out perpendicular to the side of the central

two 72-inch posts for the outer end of the parallel bars are centered 68½ inches directly beyond the two ladder support poles.

After digging footing holes and placing posts, install metal bars between posts and secure them. Check that bars are level and aligned, and make necessary adjustments. Use a string and stakes to align the row of posts. Then, nail 1 by 2 braces to the posts in order to stabilize the fitness array before pouring concrete. (See detail on page 21.) Allow two days for concrete to set.

Make the seesaw

For the seesaw, select a 2 by 10 vertical grain fir board 120 inches long. Be sure board is structurally sound, and free from splits, cracks, checks, or large knots. For appearance, choose a *flat* board.

Using a compass or a tack tied to a string, draw two circles at each end of the board, as illustrated in Figure G. Bridge these two circles with short concave sections, as shown, and cut pattern with a saber saw. Round off edges with sandpaper or a rasp.

Cut two 8-inch cleats from 1 by 2 stock, and attach them with two carriage bolts per cleat, using washers and cap nuts on the bottom (no counterbores).

Make a tent top

The tent top shown in the photograph at the beginning of this project is a single sheet of rip-stop nylon. The finished size is 41 inches wide by 129 inches long. Sew a 1-inch hem along each 129-inch side. Sew a channel, containing two 60-inch nylon cords, along each 41-inch side (Figure H). Tack cords at corners to keep them in place. Use cords to tie tent top to hardwood dowel rungs. Cauterize or glue the ends of cords to keep them from fraying.

Figure G Building seesaw

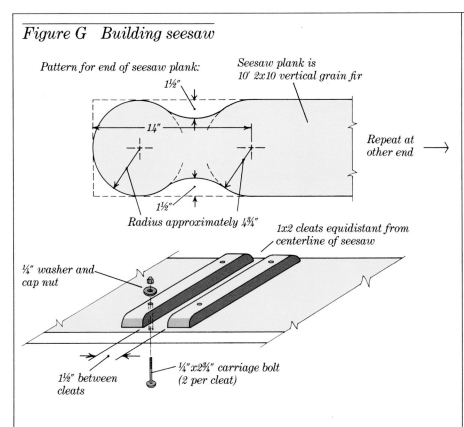

Pattern for end of seesaw plank:

1½"

14"

1½"

Radius approximately 4¾"

Seesaw plank is
10' 2x10 vertical grain fir

Repeat at
other end →

1x2 cleats equidistant from
centerline of seesaw

¼" washer and
cap nut

1½" between
cleats

¼"x2¾" carriage bolt
(2 per cleat)

Figure H   Making tent top

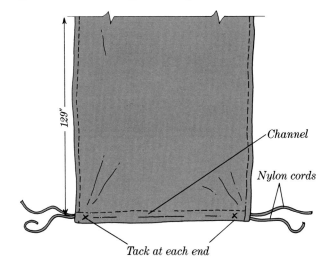

129"

Channel

Nylon cords

Tack at each end

Add a swing beam

A swing beam is a popular part of
any play structure. The swing beam
shown in the photographs and
drawings of this play structure also
appears as part of the Creative
Climber project on page 76. You will
find instructions there on how to
build and install it.

Add the add-ons

The Fitness Gym can be equipped
with a fire pole and a slide. The fire
pole is part of the Creative Climber
project on page 74, and instructions
for building slides are found on
pages 24–27. Rings and a trapeze
bar can also be added to one of the
rails on the horizontal ladder, as
shown in the photograph on pages
52–53. Order these from the manufacturers listed on page 37.

Maintenance

The Fitness Gym, like the other
projects in this section, must be
checked and tightened three months
after completion. Repair or replace
any worn or damaged parts. Repeat
the process six months later and once
a year thereafter.

Fitness Gym

Space requirements

The Fitness Gym, like the A-frame Clubhouse, may be assembled in different sizes or in phases. The illustrations on these pages show the actual size of the structures and the approximate total area required, including play safety zone, as indicated by the loop around each drawing. The smallest design is for the central structure and slide only. The medium-sized drawing includes the horizontal ladder, and the largest design includes the fitness array at the end of the horizontal ladder and the swing.

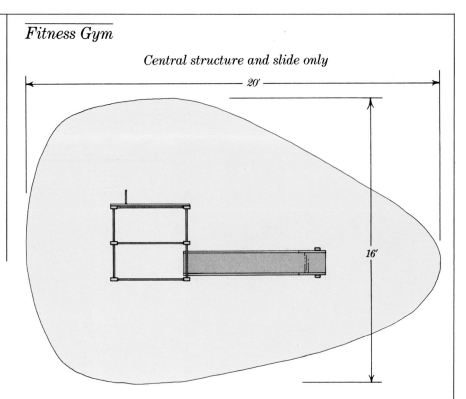

Central structure and slide only

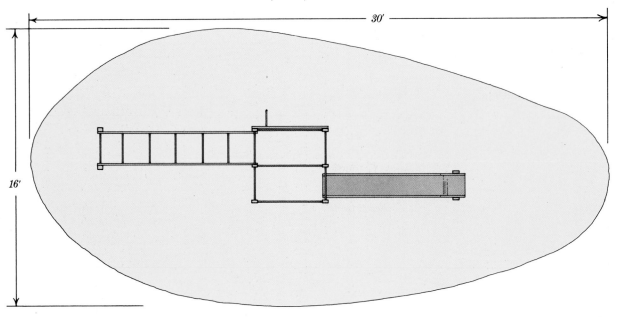

Central structure, slide, and horizontal ladder

Central structure, slide, horizontal ladder, fitness array, and swing

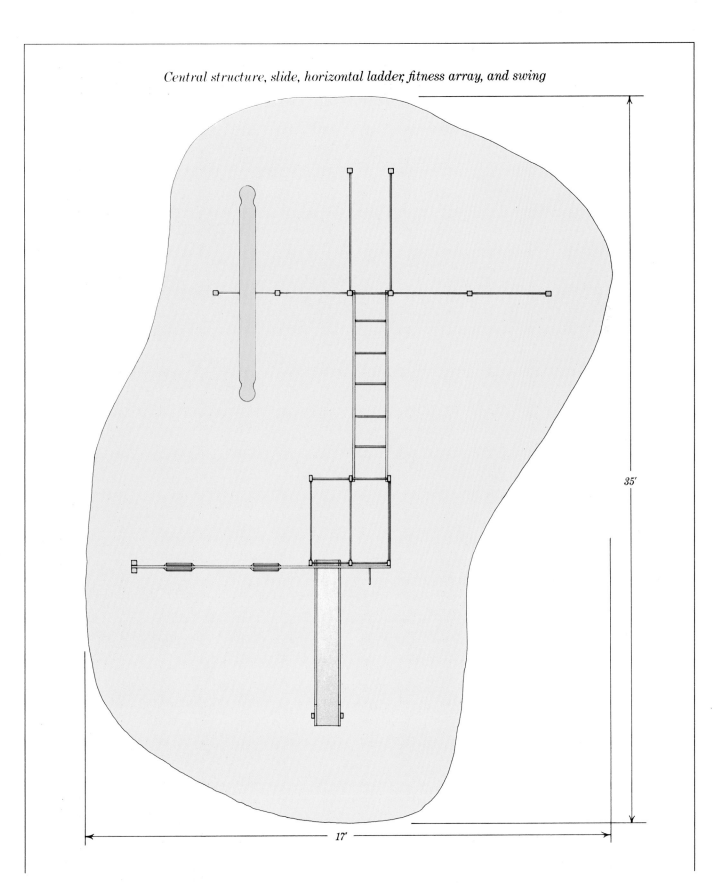

35′

17′

CREATIVE CLIMBER

T*he Creative Climber is a study in modular design. The functions of the basic core are determined by the children as they move planks, panels, and accessories to make enclosures, support platforms, tables and benches, walkways, and shelves.*

The design is also modular in that devices such as swings, horizontal ladder, trapeze, rings, fire pole, slide, net, and turning bar, even a tent top and fabric walls, can be added at any time. Look over the choices, decide on the initial configuration, and add to it in the future as you see fit. Even in its simplest arrangements the Creative Climber is an engaging structure—sure to exercise a child's mind *and* body.

The structure may be finished in bright colors as shown, or in more muted colors. If you are able to find "appearance grade" 2 by 4s, consider using a clear finish for a natural look. To ensure that the wood you choose is durable, see "Protecting wood from decay" on page 35.

The Creative Climber, like the other projects, must be checked and tightened three months after completion. Repair or replace any worn or damaged parts. Repeat the process six months later and a once a year thereafter.

The Creative Climber provides a large central structure with movable planks that children can shift and rearrange to create new spaces. Fitness equipment, slide, fire pole, and swing beam can also be added to the structure.

Creative Climber

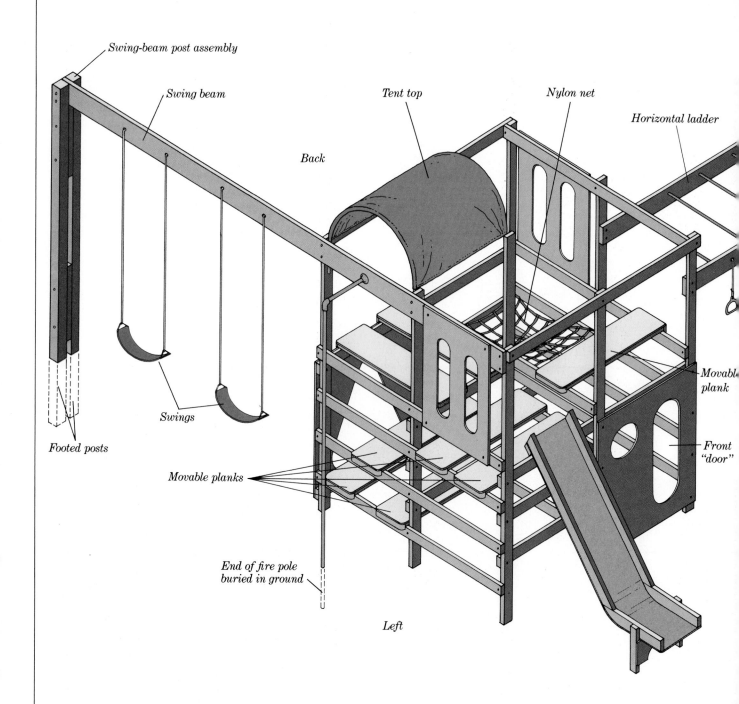

Creative Climber

Swing-beam post assembly

Swing beam

Tent top

Nylon net

Horizontal ladder

Back

Footed posts

Swings

Movabl plank

Front "door"

Movable planks

End of fire pole buried in ground

Left

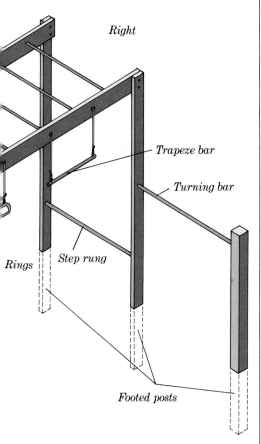

Right

Trapeze bar

Turning bar

Rings

Step rung

Footed posts

Front

Materials list

Subframes

2x4 fir
9 pieces 96" long for
  subframe vertical posts
12 pieces 80½" long for subframe rails

Hardware and miscellaneous
39 carriage bolts ¼"x5"; washers, nuts

Frame structure

2x4 fir
7 pieces 82½" long for cross rails
6 pieces 43" long for cross rails
1 piece 80½" long for top rail

Hardware and miscellaneous
21 carriage bolts ¼"x3"; washers, nuts
12 carriage bolts ¼"x3½"; washers, nuts

Panels

½" ACX plywood
1 piece 44½"x48" for lower panel
1 piece 43"x48" for lower panel
2 pieces 30"x41½" for upper panels

Hardware and miscellaneous
14 carriage bolts ¼"x2"; washers, nuts

Planks

½" ACX plywood
8 pieces 12"x45" for plank tops

1x2 pine or fir
16 pieces 42" long for plank rails

2x2 fir
16 pieces 12" long for plank cleats

Hardware and miscellaneous
128 galvanized multipurpose
  screws 1"x#6
64 galvanized multipurpose
  screws 1½"x#6
16 oz bottle waterproof glue

Fire pole

Hardware and miscellaneous
1 galvanized floor flange 1" dia
1 galvanized 90° pipe elbow 1" dia
1 galvanized nipple 1"dia x 16"
1 piece schedule 40 galvanized iron pipe
  1"dia x 108" long, one end threaded
4 machine bolts ¼"x2"; washers, nuts
Ready-mixed concrete: See "Footings"
  on pages 34–35 for amount needed

Horizontal ladder and turning bar

2x6 fir
2 pieces 96" long for ladder rails

2x4 fir
2 pieces 98½" long for
  ladder support posts

4x4 fir
1 piece 66" long for turning bar post

**¾" dia schedule 40 galvanized
  iron pipe, unthreaded**
6 pieces 37½" long for ladder rungs
1 piece 48" long for turning bar
1 piece 39½" long for step rung

Hardware and miscellaneous
12 HDG nails 16d
8 carriage bolts ¼"x3"; washers, nuts
Ready-mixed concrete: See "Footings"
  on pages 34–35 for amount needed

Swing beam

**2x8 select structural douglas fir
  (4x8 if other species or grade)**
1 piece 16' long for swing beam

**4x4 fir, redwood, or
  pressure-treated wood**
2 pieces 114" long for swing beam posts

2x4 fir
2 pieces 24" long for post blocks

Hardware and miscellaneous
6 carriage bolts ¼"x5"; washers, nuts
6 machine bolts ⅜"x9"; washers, nuts
Ready-mixed concrete: See "Footings"
  on pages 34–35 for amount needed

Tent top and sides

Hardware and miscellaneous
1 piece rip-stop nylon
  45"x57½" for tent top
3 pieces rip-stop nylon
  37"x38" for tent walls
2 pieces schedule 20 PVC pipe
  ¾"dia x 74" for tent loops
8 pipe clamps ¾" dia for tent holders
16 self-tapping pan-head
  wood screws 1"x#8 for tent holders
1 spool nylon or polyester thread
6 Bungee stretch cords 41" long
  with hooks for wall attachment

Tools needed
Carpenter's square and level (or combination square); 25' tape measure; hammer; handsaw or circular saw; saber saw;
wood rasp or coarse sandpaper; screw
driver (electric preferred with #2 Phillips
bit); electric drill; ¼", ³⁄₁₆", ⅜", and ¾"
drill bits (for counterbores) and 1" drill
bits (for rungs); ⁷⁄₁₆" and ⁹⁄₁₆" ratchet and
sockets; ¾" and 1" spade bits; four 8-inch
C-clamps

Creative Climber

Construction steps

Organize work space. Set out materials and tools. Be certain that safety precautions have been taken, extension cords in good order, work surfaces secured, and so on. Check Figures A-1 through A-9 to familiarize yourself with the types of connections used on the Creative Climber.

Figure A-1 2 flat 2-bys

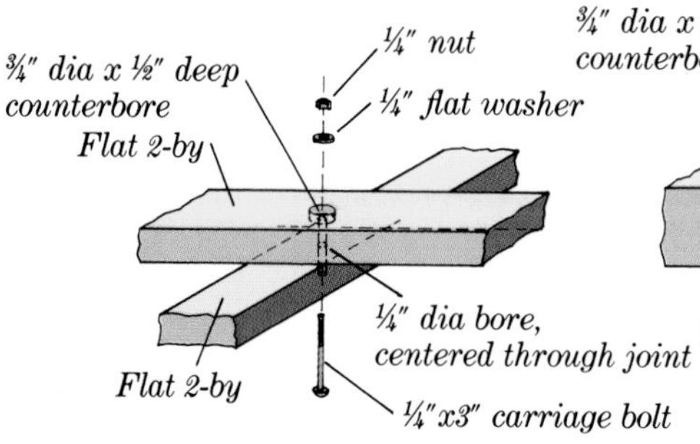

¼" nut
¾" dia x ½" deep counterbore
¼" flat washer
Flat 2-by
¼" dia bore, centered through joint
Flat 2-by
¼"x3" carriage bolt

Figure A-2 2-by to 4-by or 2-by to 2x4 on edge

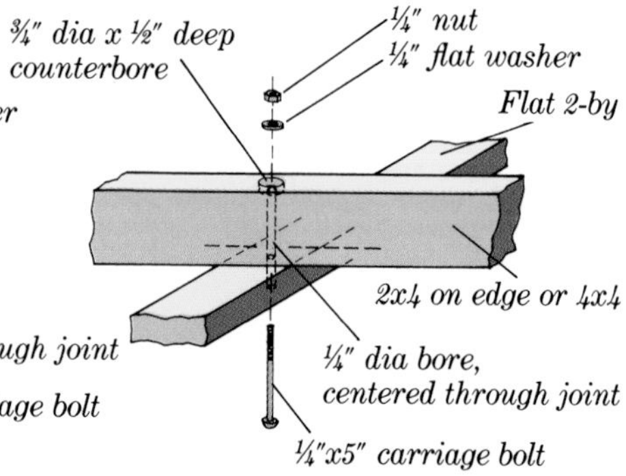

¾" dia x ½" deep counterbore
¼" nut
¼" flat washer
Flat 2-by
2x4 on edge or 4x4
¼" dia bore, centered through joint
¼"x5" carriage bolt

Connections to ½" plywood sheet

Figure A-3 A-4 A-5 A-6

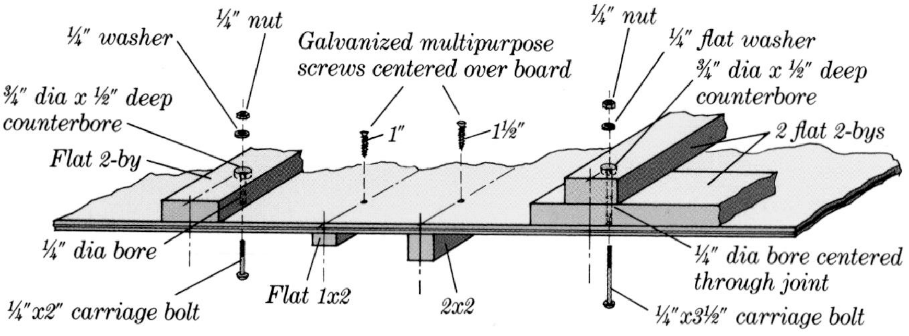

¼" washer
¼" nut
Galvanized multipurpose screws centered over board
¼" nut
¼" flat washer
¾" dia x ½" deep counterbore
¾" dia x ½" deep counterbore
1"
1½"
2 flat 2-bys
Flat 2-by
¼" dia bore
¼"x2" carriage bolt
Flat 1x2
2x2
¼" dia bore centered through joint
¼"x3½" carriage bolt

Figure A-7 Connecting swing beam to post

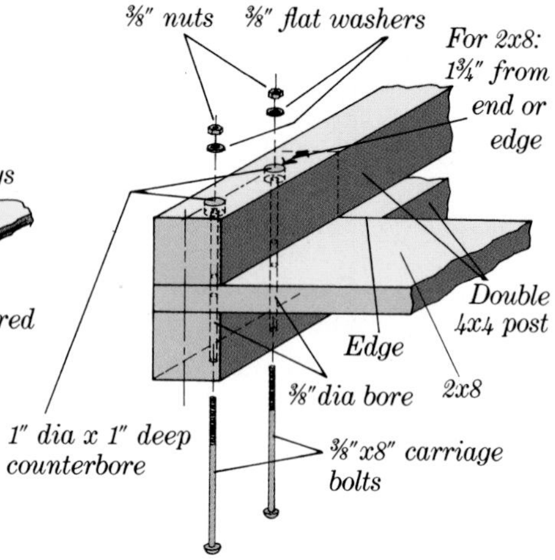

⅜" nuts
⅜" flat washers
For 2x8: 1¾" from end or edge
Double 4x4 post
Edge
⅜"dia bore
2x8
1" dia x 1" deep counterbore
⅜"x8" carriage bolts

Figure A-8 Connecting swing beam to main structure

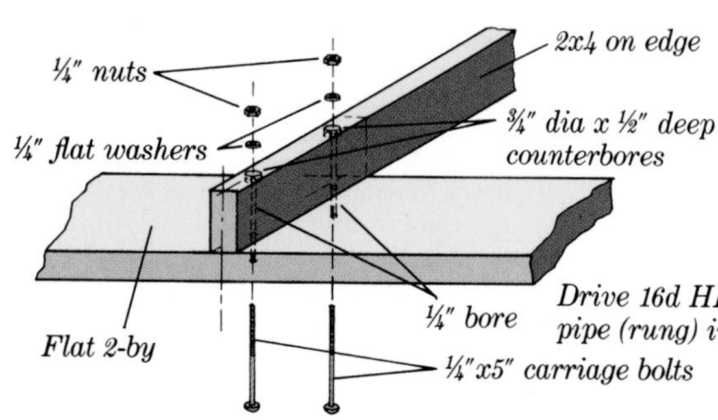

2x4 on edge
¼" nuts
¾" dia x ½" deep counterbores
¼" flat washers
Flat 2-by
¼" bore
¼"x5" carriage bolts

Drive 16d HDG nail to hold pipe (rung) in position

Figure A-9 Horizontal-ladder rung attachment

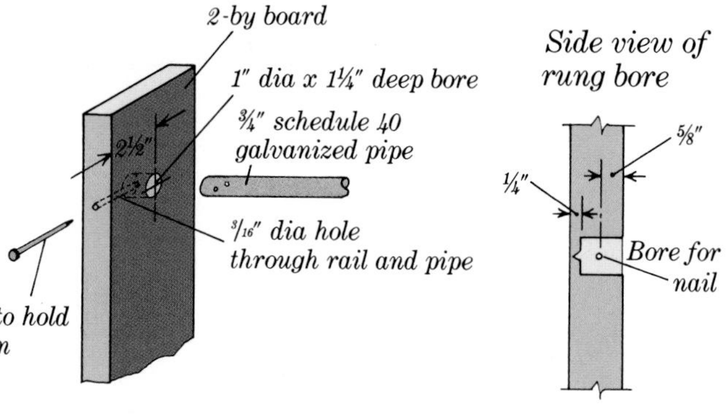

2-by board
1" dia x 1¼" deep bore
2½"
¾" schedule 40 galvanized pipe
5/16" dia hole through rail and pipe
Side view of rung bore
⅝"
¼"
Bore for nail

Construct the three subframes

Each of the three subframes is the same, consisting of three vertical posts each 96 inches long, and four rails each 80½ inches long. Since the posts rest on the ground, the bottom 4 inches must be treated with wood preservative. To treat them, you can dip the ends into a bucket containing preservative.

Lay out and drill each post as shown in Figure B. Use of a drill guide is recommended to ensure that counterbores and holes are straight and centered on the boards.

With rails supported on blocks, position posts on top of them. Align the outside edges of the outside posts with the ends of the rails. Locate the middle post in the center of each rail so that it is precisely halfway between the outer posts. Complete the ¼-inch holes through rails (see Figure C). Complete each subframe by feeding 5-inch carriage bolts from underneath and threading on nuts from the top. Refer to Figure A-2 for connection specifications. Check that diagonal measures are equal before tightening all nuts.

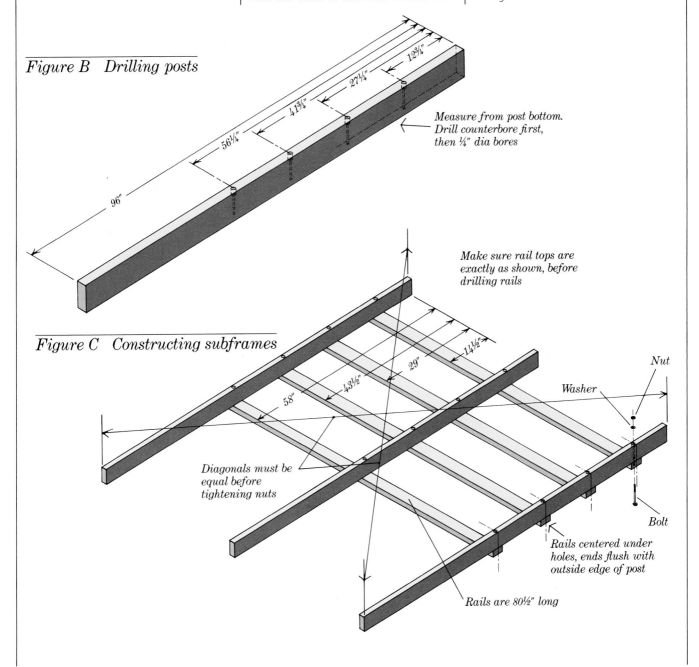

Figure B   Drilling posts

12¾"
27¼"
41¾"
56¼"
96"

Measure from post bottom.
Drill counterbore first,
then ¼" dia bores

Make sure rail tops are
exactly as shown, before
drilling rails

Figure C   Constructing subframes

11½"
29"
43½"
58"

Nut
Washer
Bolt

Diagonals must be
equal before
tightening nuts

Rails centered under
holes, ends flush with
outside edge of post

Rails are 80½" long

Creative Climber

Assemble the main structure

Since the movable planks of the Creative Climber must fit either crosswise or lengthwise anywhere within the structure, it is important to assemble the subframe and cross rails exactly as shown in Figure D. It now becomes important to note which sides are the front, right, back, and left. Note that the tops of the already connected subframe rails will not be at the same levels as the tops of the cross rails, which will be connected next. This enables planks placed crosswise to clear any planks placed lengthwise.

Begin assembly by cutting the cross rails as follows: seven at 82½ inches long and six at 43 inches long. Mark the position of the tops of the cross rails on the sides of the vertical subframe posts that face the back of the structure. Use the measurements shown in Figure D. Next, mark the midpoint of the long cross rails (41¼ inches from either end). Then, with the help of an assistant or two, stand up one of the subframes and clamp a middle cross rail to it. Stand up the center subframe and clamp it to the midpoint of the same rail (Figure D). With C-clamps holding subframes and cross rail together, drill connections as shown in Figure A-1 and fit bolts. (You can only drill as many connections as you have C-clamps; you may want to borrow a few.)

Continue accurately fitting cross rails to subframes until you have completed the structure. Note that all cross rails bolt to the back side of subframe posts except for the one across the top of the front side. This bolts to the outside of the front. Note also that 3½-inch (rather than 3-inch) bolts are used where the lower panels attach to the main structure at the cross-rail junctions. See Figure G, page 72, for locations.

Figure E shows a rail across the top of the right side of the subframe. This 80½-inch rail can be fitted now. There is no front-to-back rail at the top of the center subframe, and the rail at the top of the left subframe is omitted because the swing beam will attach to that position.

Figure D   Assembling subframes and cross rails

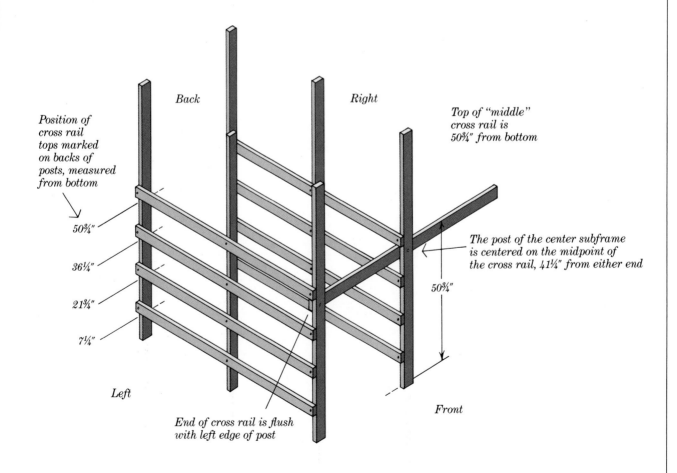

Back

Right

Top of "middle" cross rail is 50¾" from bottom

Position of cross rail tops marked on backs of posts, measured from bottom

50¾"

36¼"

21¾"

7¼"

The post of the center subframe is centered on the midpoint of the cross rail, 41¼" from either end

50¾"

Left

End of cross rail is flush with left edge of post

Front

Figure E Adding cross rails

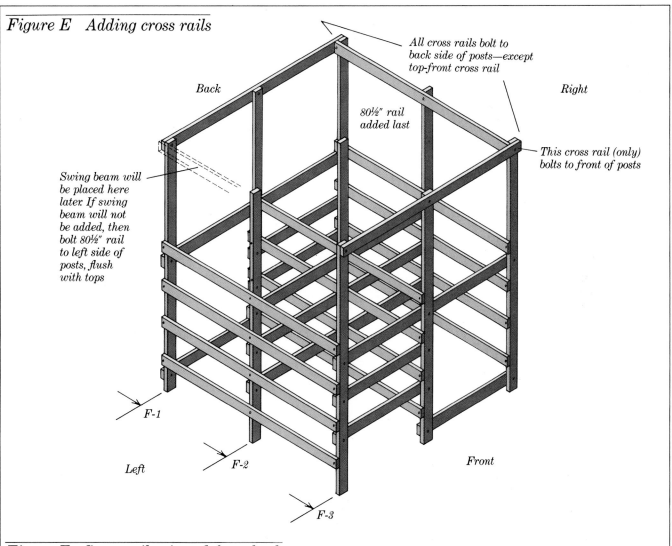

All cross rails bolt to back side of posts—except top-front cross rail

Back

Right

80½" rail added last

This cross rail (only) bolts to front of posts

Swing beam will be placed here later. If swing beam will not be added, then bolt 80½" rail to left side of posts, flush with tops

F-1

F-2

Left

F-3

Front

Figure F Cross rails viewed from back

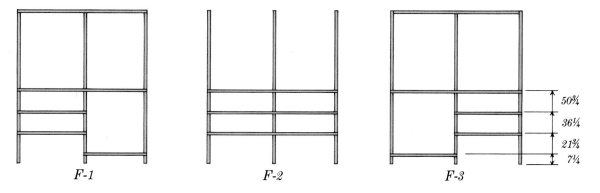

F-1

F-2

F-3

50¾

36¼

21¾

7¼

Creative Climber

Add plywood panels

The plywood panels are required on the Creative Climber for structural rigidity. Without the panels, the whole structure would eventually start to wobble and sway. The panels also add enclosed areas and soften the appearance by incorporating curved lines.

The four structural panels can be cut from two standard 4 by 8 plywood sheets. Cut the two panels for the lower level from the first sheet. Figure H shows the layout for these panels as well as the layout for the upper two panels, which are cut from the second sheet of plywood. Since the upper panels are smaller, you will have plywood left to make the slide. Also save the cutout pieces.

Circles and curved shapes can be marked on plywood with string, nail, and pencil. Tie a 1-inch loop in one end of the string. Tap nail into the center of circle, and tie the other end of string to nail. Use loop to guide pencil in a circle (see Figure H).

After cutting out the plywood panels and shapes, but before assembly, consider painting the panels as well as the central structure—especially if you have decided to use several different finishes. Also, before attaching the panels, carefully level the structure. To do this you may have to remove the earth under some of the posts.

Follow Figure G for placement of panels, using connections shown on Figure A-3 (page 68). Remove previously installed 3½-inch bolts located along the sides of the lower panels. If you plan to add the swing beam, the left panel will have to wait until beam is in place.

Note: The movable planks will fit more easily if you place two extra washers on each bolt of the front panel. Place them *between* the panel and its posts.

Figure G Placing panels

Secure to Split-level Playhouse with two 3" x #10 round-head screws through 2x4s into rail. When moving playhouse structure, remove these screws and move slide assembly separately

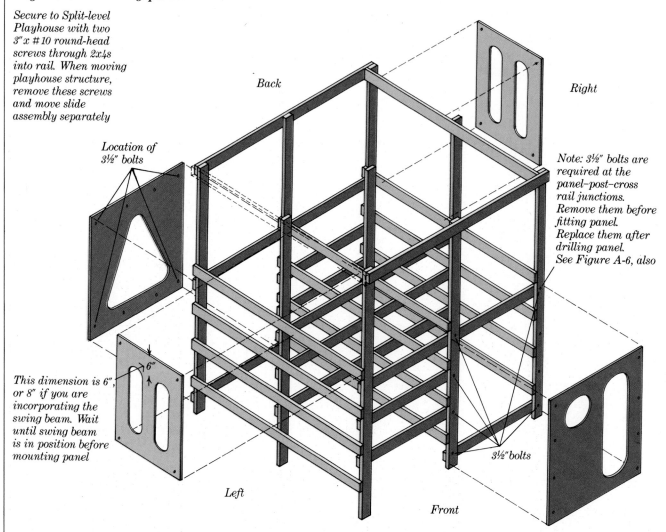

Back

Right

Location of 3½" bolts

Note: 3½" bolts are required at the panel–post–cross rail junctions. Remove them before fitting panel. Replace them after drilling panel. See Figure A-6, also

This dimension is 6", or 8" if you are incorporating the swing beam. Wait until swing beam is in position before mounting panel

6"

3½" bolts

Left

Front

Figure H   Layout of plywood panels

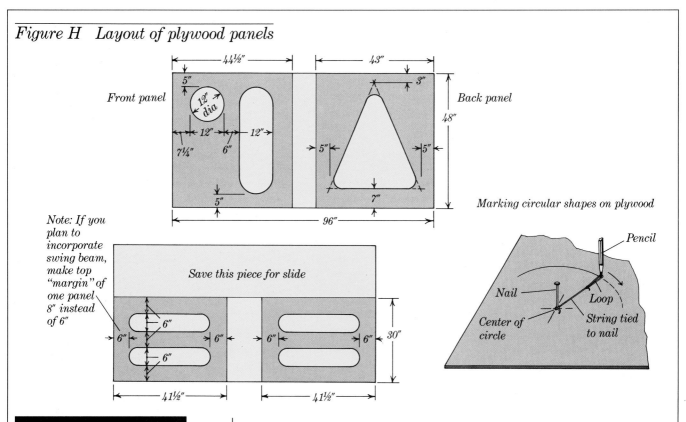

Front panel

44½"

5"

12" dia

12"   12"

7¼"   6"

5"

43"

3"

Back panel

48"

5"   5"

7"

96"

Marking circular shapes on plywood

Pencil

Nail   Loop

Center of   String tied
circle   to nail

Note: If you
plan to
incorporate
swing beam,
make top
"margin" of
one panel
8" instead
of 6"

Save this piece for slide

6"   6"   6"   6"

6"   6"

6"   6"

30"

41½"   41½"

Make the deck planks

Each of the eight planks consists of a
12-inch by 45-inch plywood top supported by two 42-inch-long 1 by 2
rails and held in place by two 12-
inch-long 2 by 2 cleats. Assemble
tops and support rails using waterproof glue and eight 1-inch by No. 6
galvanized multipurpose screws per
side, spaced every 5¾ inches (with a
⅞-inch space at each end). See Figure A-4. Rails are mounted flush with
the outside edge of the plywood. The
screws are designed to be self-coun-
tersinking, but this requires a bit of
effort on the last turn.

Next, glue and screw the cleats to
the plywood using 1½-inch multipurpose galvanized screws, four per
cleat. See Figure A-5.

To finish planks, first round off
edges with medium sandpaper or a
rasp. The four vertical outside corners should be rounded, using a rasp
or a router. Finally, sand, prime, and
paint each entire plank with a durable finish.

Figure I   Assembling deck planks

1" screws

1½" screws

Plywood top

Radius
outside
vertical
corners

1x2 rail

2x2 cleat

Must be 42"
(inside-to-inside)

Add the fire pole

The fire pole attaches to the top rail of the left subframe. This top rail is made from a 2 by 4 or is an extension of the 2 by 8 swing beam. If you plan to add the swing beam, you must do so before adding the fire pole.

The first step is to assemble the component parts of the pole. Screw the elbow onto the threaded end of the 108-inch pipe, then thread the 16-inch nipple into the elbow, and

Figure J   Adding fire pole

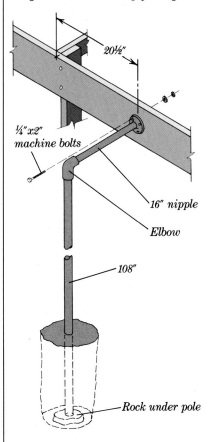

20½"

¼"x2" machine bolts

16" nipple

Elbow

108"

Rock under pole

the flange onto the nipple. The illustration on page 66 shows the location recommended for the pole.

The flange attaches to the top rail, centered top to bottom, and at a point 20½ inches forward from the back of the back post. Before trying to bolt the flange, dig the hole for the bottom of the pole. The hole should be centered at a point 20½ inches forward from the back of the back post and 18 inches out from the left side of the structure. Place bottom of pole into hole, then mark, drill, and bolt flange to structure using four ¼-inch by 2-inch machine bolts. Cement or a 3-inch to 4-inch stone placed under pole will make it more solid after hole is filled and compacted.

Add the horizontal ladder and turning bar

The main rails of the horizontal ladder are made from 2 by 6 stock. Select two straight 8-foot lengths of fir that are free from large knots, splits, cracks, or checks. The rails are supported at one end by the main structure and at the outer end by two footed 2 by 4 posts. Use two bolts at each rail and post connection. Check Figure A-1 (page 68) for drilling and bolt specifications. Apply wood preservative to lower portion of posts or use pressure-treated posts.

Cut outer posts to a length of 98½ inches each. This will yield a footing depth of 18 inches and a rung height of 78 inches. Cut posts for turning bar to a length of 66 inches, which will give a turning bar height of 42 inches.

After cutting all stock to length, lay out and drill holes for rungs. Holes do not extend completely through rails (or posts). Specifications for rung connection using 16d HDG nails are detailed in Figure A-9, page 68. Figure K shows locations of connections. Assemble rungs and rails to make ladder. Fit the step rung between the two ladder posts and secure it.

Dig footing holes at least 18 inches deep and centered at 90¾ inches to the right of the main structure (directly to the right of front and middle posts). The footing hole for the turning-bar post is centered 46¼ inches directly in front of the hole for the front ladder support post.

After applying preservative to the bottoms of the posts, tip ladder support-post assembly into footing holes. With the help of assistants, lift ladder assembly into position and secure it between the four posts with four C-clamps. Make sure that the whole assembly is plumb and level, and adjust if necessary. Attach ladder assembly to posts using two ¼-inch by 3-inch bolts per connection, spaced 3 inches apart and centered between edges of overlapping boards. Figure A-1 shows bolt and drilling sizes.

Drill turning-bar post and front ladder support post to accept turning bar. Apply preservative to bottom of post, place post into the hole, and fasten turning-bar pipe (Figure A-9). After making sure that assemblies are level and plumb, put concrete into footing holes. (See "Footings" on pages 34–35 for more information on this process.)

Accessories such as rings and a trapeze bar can be added along one of the rails of the horizontal ladder (as shown in the illustration on the right). Consult the list of commercial sources on page 37 for suppliers. Be sure to follow the instructions provided by the manufacturer when assembling and attaching these accessories.

Figure K   Assembling horizontal ladder

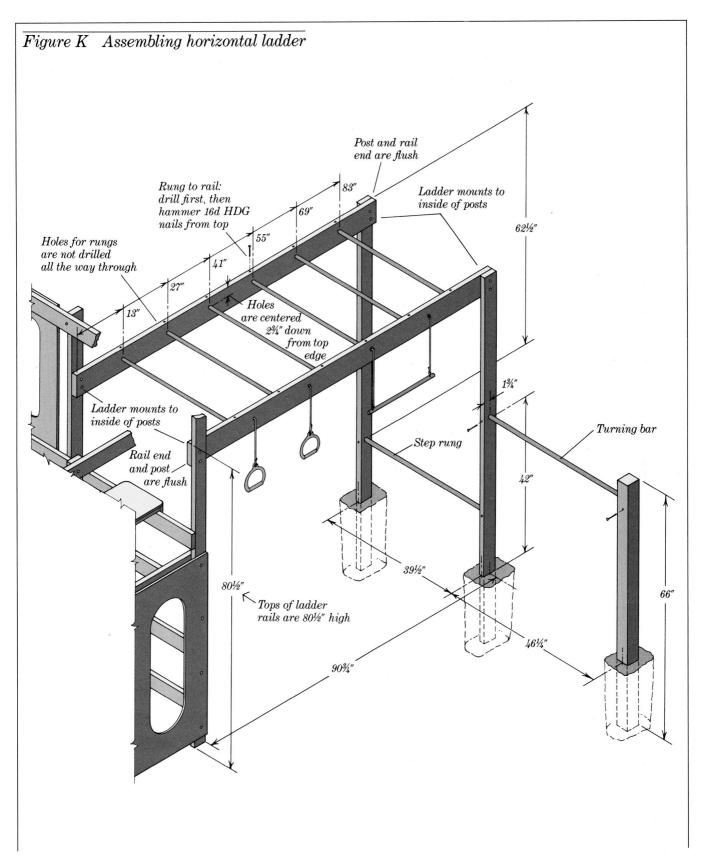

Post and rail
end are flush

Rung to rail:
drill first, then
hammer 16d HDG
nails from top

Ladder mounts to
inside of posts

83"

69"

55"

41"

27"

13"

Holes for rungs
are not drilled
all the way through

62½"

Holes
are centered
2¾" down
from top
edge

Ladder mounts to
inside of posts

1¾"

Turning bar

Rail end
and post
are flush

Step rung

42"

80½"

Tops of ladder
rails are 80½" high

39½"

66"

46¼"

90¾"

Creative Climber

Add the swing beam

Because the swing beam itself is 16 feet long and subject to stress, select it carefully. Choose fir that is free from large knots, checks, splits, cracks, warping, or twisting. If you cannot locate a ''select structural'' grade of 2 by 8, use a 3 by 8 or 4 by 8 instead, and alter the space blocks accordingly. The lower 30 inches of each 4 by 4 post must be treated with wood preservative. Alternatively, it is possible to buy pressure-treated posts. Ten-foot posts require a 24-inch-deep footing; 114-inch posts an 18-inch-deep footing.

Drill and bolt the two 4 by 4 posts and the 2 by 4 blocks together (see Figure A-7) to form the post assembly, as shown in Figure L. Before tightening nuts down completely, fit end of swing beam into top of post assembly. Use a carpenter's square to create a right angle between post assembly and beam, then drill and bolt pieces together. All bolts passing through the post assembly are ⅜-inch by 9-inch machine bolts. Unlike the carriage bolts used elsewhere on this project, the machine bolts will need a flat washer under the head as well as a washer under the nut. Use a 1-inch bit to make counterbores for the nut side of the bolts. Grip hex-heads with wrench or pliers to keep bolts from turning as you tighten nuts.

Dig the footing hole centered around a point 110 inches straight back from the left-rear corner of the structure. A footing depth of at least 18 inches is required. With the help of assistants, ease post assembly into hole while raising beam into position. Clamp the beam to the tops of the main structure posts and check that the swing-beam is level and plumb.

Drill and bolt swing beam to main structure posts using two 5-inch carriage bolts per post, spaced 1 inch from top and 1½ inches from bottom of swing beam (see Figure A-8). Fill post hole with concrete and do not allow anyone to touch the structure until concrete has set. Finally, attach the left plywood panel to the subframe rail and swing beam (Figure G, page 72).

Select the swings

Many swings and fittings can be used on this swing beam. The swings section on pages 22–23 gives instructions for building your own, or you can consult the list of sources for playground equipment on page 37.

Figure L   Building swing beam

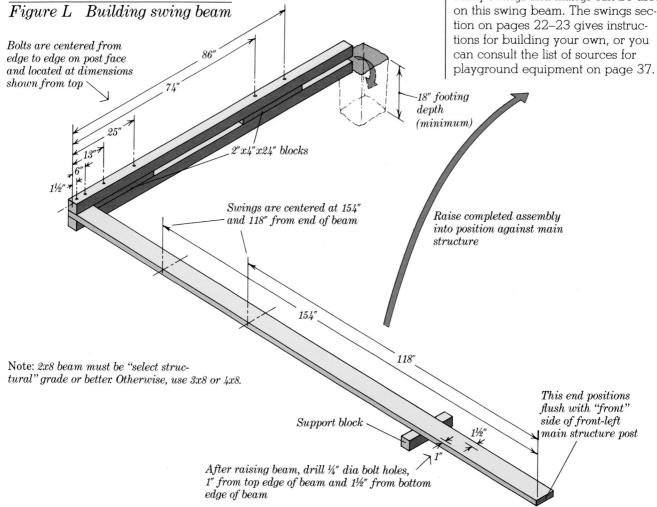

Bolts are centered from edge to edge on post face and located at dimensions shown from top

86"
74"
25"
13"
6"
1½"

2"x4"x24" blocks

18" footing depth (minimum)

Swings are centered at 154" and 118" from end of beam

Raise completed assembly into position against main structure

154"
118"

Note: 2x8 beam must be "select structural" grade or better. Otherwise, use 3x8 or 4x8.

Support block

This end positions flush with "front" side of front-left main structure post

1½"
1"

After raising beam, drill ¼" dia bolt holes, 1" from top edge of beam and 1½" from bottom edge of beam

Add a tent top

Loosely screw the eight pipe clamps to the inside of the posts where you will mount tent top, as shown in Figure M. Cut rip-stop nylon to a shape of 45 inches by 57½ inches. Fold over ½ inch of each short side and sew a hem. Next, fold over 2 inches of each long side and sew channel for the pipe. Cut two pieces of PVC pipe to 74 inches each, and slide a pipe through each channel of the nylon so that about 9 inches of pipe protrude from each end of channel. Insert one end of each pipe into the loose pipe clamps on the posts, and bend pipe and fabric over to create a tent. Slide the other ends of pipe into the two opposing pipe clamps, and tighten all clamps down.

Make fabric wall panels

The three movable fabric tent walls are made from 37-inch by 38-inch rip-stop nylon. Sew a ½-inch hem along each short side, then fold 1 inch of each long side over a stretch cord and sew a channel (with cord inside). Using a needle and thread, tack center of cord to center of channel to keep cord in place. (See Figure N.) This will result in 36-inch-square panels, with hooks at the corners for attaching to the structure.

Add the net

The nylon webbing net shown in the photographs and illustration at the beginning of the Creative Climber section requires special design and construction techniques. It is available in a size to fit this structure from Olympic Recreation, which is listed with other playground-equipment manufacturers on page 37.

Add the slide

See the section on slides on pages 24–27 for information on constructing and attaching a slide to the Creative Climber.

Figure M   Assembling tent top

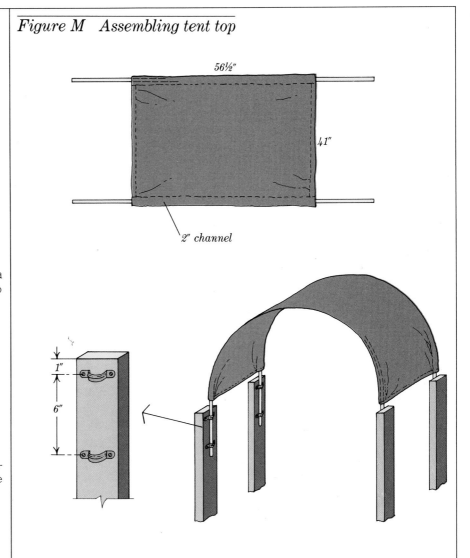

56½"

41"

2" channel

1"

6"

Figure N   Sewing fabric tent walls

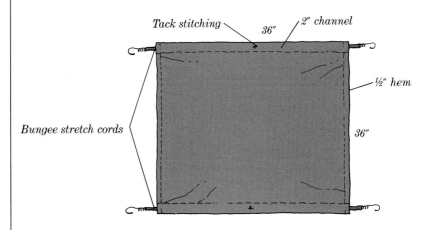

Tack stitching

36"

2" channel

½" hem

Bungee stretch cords

36"

Creative Climber

Space requirements

The Creative Climber is a flexible design that allows for many different configurations. The main structure could even be constructed in a half-size format that would measure only 43 inches by 84 inches. At the other extreme, you could build a six-square unit instead of the four-square climber detailed here.

The illustrations on these pages show the actual size of the structures and the approximate total area required, including a play safety zone as indicated by the loop around each drawing. The smallest design shows the basic structure with the slide. The medium-sized drawing includes the horizontal ladder, and the swing is added in the largest design.

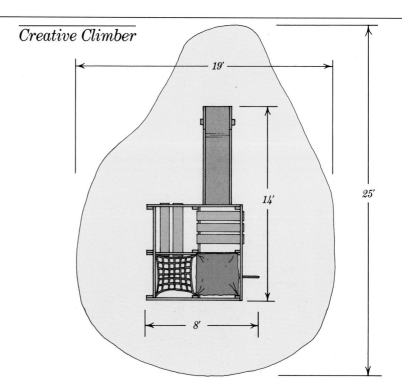

Creative Climber

Creative Climber with slide

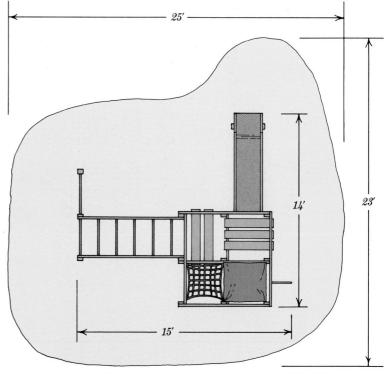

Creative Climber with slide and horizontal ladder

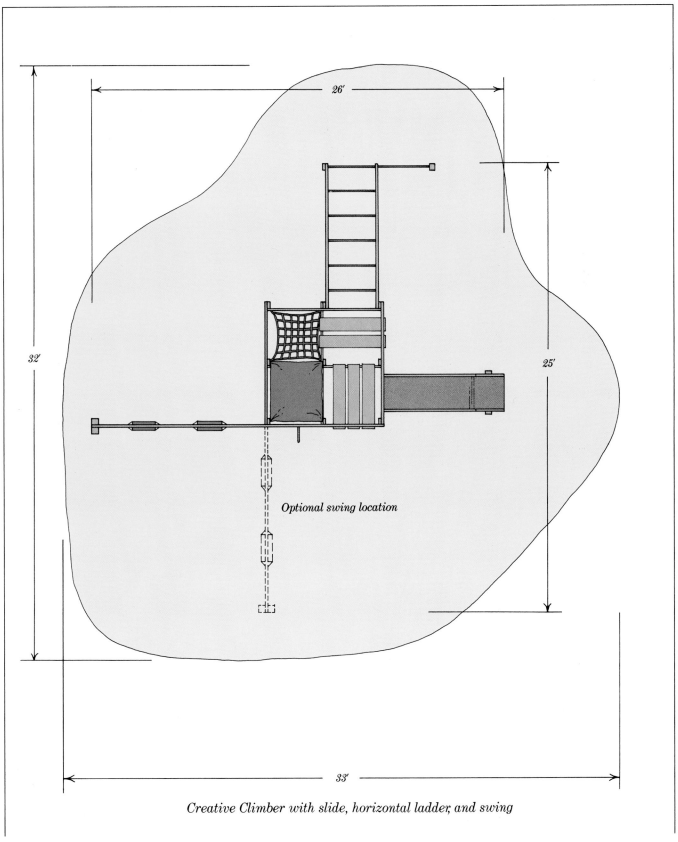

26'

32'

25'

Optional swing location

33'

Creative Climber with slide, horizontal ladder, and swing

SPLIT-LEVEL PLAYHOUSE

T he Split-level playhouse is the most architectural of the designs in this book, and, of all the structures, it looks most like a traditional playhouse. You can even choose the finishing materials to complement your residence. Children will appreciate the variety of spaces created by the split-level decks, as well as the activity provided by the ladders and other peripherals.

Basic carpentry skills are required for construction of this playhouse. Dimensions of the structure are given, but because actual dimensions of lumberyard lumber vary a bit, individual board dimensions rarely are given. Since the playhouse is an unweatherized outdoor structure, it is necessary to use galvanized or plated nails, screws, and bolts. Also, read "Protecting wood from decay" on page 35 for information and guidelines on wood preservation.

As you look at the illustrations, it is important to note which side is marked front, back, left, and right. This orientation is maintained throughout. The playhouse itself is constructed in three distinct stages: the framing stage, utilizing 2 by 4s; the siding stage, utilizing plywood; and the trim stage, utilizing 1 by 4 and 1 by 6 trim.

All children want a special "house" to play in. The Split-level Playhouse also includes a swing beam, a wave slide, and a fire pole in the back as an alternate exit from the upper level.

Split-level Playhouse

Construct the subframes

The framing of the Split-level Playhouse consists of a front wall subframe and a back wall subframe. Later, these will be connected by a number of crosspieces.

Build subframes on a hard, flat, level surface—a patio or a driveway. Observe dimensions shown in Figures A and B. Use standard framing procedures: 16d nails for facenail connections and 8d nails for toenail connections.

Figure A shows all the critical dimensions, which, if followed, will result in roof angles of 30 degrees.

The two decks that make up the second floor are supported, in part, by ledger boards nailed to the insides of the front and back wall subframes. Since the decking is ½-inch plywood, the tops of the ledgers (and supporting crosspieces) must be at a height of 59½ inches for the upper deck and 47½ inches for the lower deck. The blocking within the wall framing adjacent to the ledgers, however, is even with the top of the decking—at 60 and 48 inches, respectively.

Split-level Playhouse

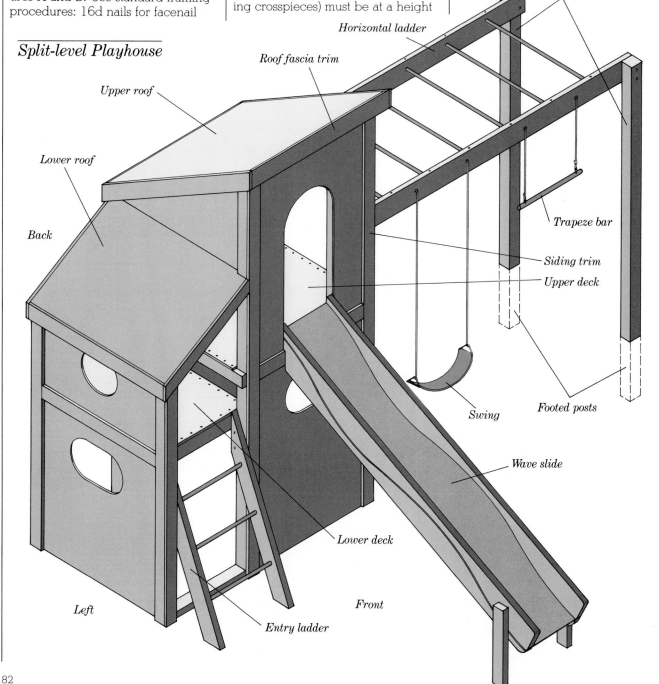

Upper roof

Lower roof

Back

Left

Entry ladder

Roof fascia trim

Horizontal ladder

Support posts

Trapeze bar

Siding trim

Upper deck

Footed posts

Swing

Wave slide

Lower deck

Front

Materials list

Subframe assemblies

2x4 fir
4 pieces 120" long for tall-side studs
4 pieces 96" long for short-side studs, base plates
5 pieces 72" long for short studs, cripples
5 pieces 48" long for top plates, center plate ledgers
5 pieces 36" long for studs, plates, ledgers
1 piece 24" long for blocking
2 pieces 12" long for blocking

Structure framing

2x4 fir
7 pieces 48" long for crosspieces
3 pieces 72" long for upper rafters
3 pieces 36" long for lower rafters
1 piece 36" long for "last stud"

¾" dia schedule 40 galvanized iron pipe, unthreaded
3 pieces 41" long for cross rungs

Floors and walls

2x4 fir
2 pieces 48" long for floor joists
2 pieces 36" long for floor joists

Floors and walls continued

2x2 fir
2 pieces 48" long for nailing frame
2 pieces 36" long for nailing frame

½" ACX plywood
1 piece 4x8 for decking

⅜" cedar siding plywood*
1 piece 4x8 for roof
4 pieces 4x8 for walls

Entry ladder

2x4 fir
2 pieces 72" long for rails

¾" dia schedule 40 galvanized iron pipe, unthreaded
3 pieces 26½" long for rungs

Hardware and miscellaneous
6 lag screws ¼"x3"; washers

Horizontal ladder

2x6 select structural fir
2 pieces 96" long for rails

4x4 redwood or pressure-treated fir
2 pieces 96" long for posts

¾" dia schedule 40 galvanized iron pipe, unthreaded
6 pieces 40½" long for rungs

Hardware and miscellaneous
4 lag screws ¼"x5"; washers
4 carriage bolts ¼"x5"; washers, nuts

Trim

1x6 redwood
3 pieces 60" long for roof fascia
2 pieces 72" long for roof fascia
1 piece 96" long for roof fascia

1x4 redwood
3 pieces 72" long for siding trim
8 pieces 96" long for siding trim
4 pieces 120" long for siding trim

For overall assembly

Galvanized box nails
4 lbs of 16d
1 lb of 8d
1 lb of 6d
1 lb of 4d
24 HDG nails 16d (for rung attachment)

Miscellaneous
1 qt wood preservative (approved for safe use) for underground portion
Ready-mixed concrete: See "Footings" on pages 34–35 for amount needed.

*Note: All framing lumber must be cut to actual dimensions

Tools needed
Carpenter's square and level (or combination square); 25' tape measure; handsaw or circular saw; saber saw; wood rasp or coarse sandpaper; electric drill; hammer; protractor and sliding bevel; ⁹/₁₆" ratchet and socket; ¼" and ³/₁₆" drill bits; ¾" and 1" spade bits

Figure A   Subframe dimensions

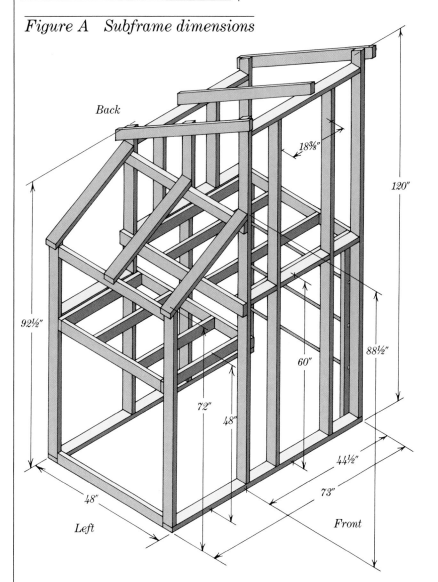

Back

18⅜"

120"

92½"

88½"

60"

72"

48"

44½"

48"

73"

Left

Front

Split-level Playhouse

The ledgers supporting the front and back of the upper deck are cut 1½-inches short at the right side to allow for the crosspiece (joist), as shown in Figure B.

Cripple studs are placed at the right ends of the front and back sub-frames. These cripple studs support the weight of the right crosspiece and are drilled for ladder rungs.

Four studs are used in the tall section of the front wall. The opening between the two inner studs must be 18⅜ inches wide to accommodate the slide.

After assembling each subframe, square it up and nail a 1 by 2 diagonal brace (or two) to the inside to maintain alignment until plywood is attached.

Prepare the site

The site for the playhouse must be level and flat. Use a shovel or rake, a 6-foot board, and a level to smooth out and check site.

Figure B   Constructing subframes

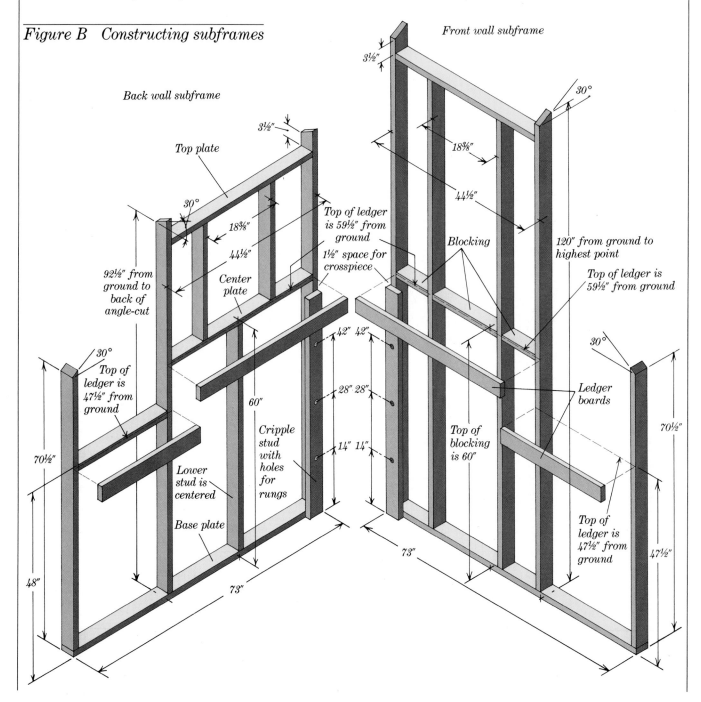

Erect the frame

Cut the seven crosspieces to length: three at 48 inches long, three at 41 inches, and one at 38 inches. Look at Figure C to see how crosspieces fit in subframes. Their position determines their length. Bevel-rip one of the 48-inch pieces to form the uppermost crosspiece, which supports the upper edge of the lower roof. The angle of the bevel is 30 degrees from horizontal (after mounting). With an assistant, carry crosspieces and subframe assemblies to the site.

Stand subframes up, insert metal cross rungs, and nail in all crosspieces. (Toenail the three pieces in the left end wall.) Drill a 3/16-inch hole, and drive a 16d HDG nail to secure each pipe rung. With structure on its leveled pad, check again that it is level and square; make any necessary corrections. Nail temporary diagonal braces to walls to maintain alignment. Position braces so they will not interfere with decking and roof.

Figure C   Erecting the frame

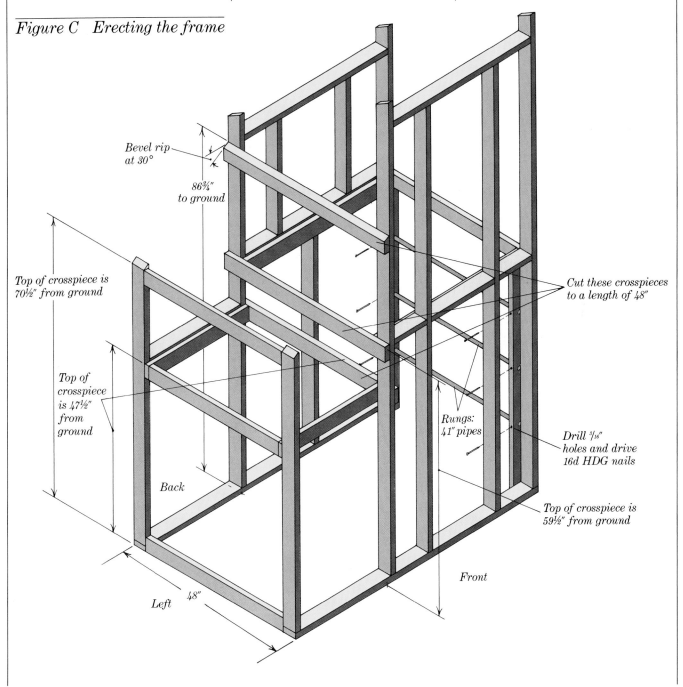

Bevel rip at 30°

86¾" to ground

Top of crosspiece is 70½" from ground

Top of crosspiece is 47½" from ground

Back

Left   48"

Cut these crosspieces to a length of 48"

Rungs: 41" pipes

Drill 3/16" holes and drive 16d HDG nails

Top of crosspiece is 59½" from ground

Front

Split-level Playhouse

Lay the decks

Fitting the rafters will be easier if you have a platform to stand on. Before laying in the plywood, place two floor joists in each deck. These joists run from left to right between the cross-pieces (Figure D). The tops of these joists, as well as the tops of the cross-pieces, must all be flush with the tops of the front and back ledger boards. Drive 16d galvanized box nails through crosspieces into ends of joists.

Cut the decking from ½-inch ACX plywood. Figure F-2 shows the layout for the plywood panels, but take actual dimensions from the structure and cut accordingly. Lay in plywood decking (see Figure E), and nail it down with 6d galvanized box nails spaced every 6 inches.

Raise the roof

Allowing for a 1½-inch overhang (see Figure D), make vertical end cuts by cutting a 60-degree angle on each end of the upper rafters. Note that these three rafters are placed *on edge*. Facenail outer rafters to the outside edges of the studs. Toenail inner rafter to the midpoints of the top plates.

Note that the lower rafters mount flat. Cut them so that the upper end of each is flush with the right edge of the beveled crosspiece (already attached), with the lower end overhanging by 1½ inches. A 60-degree angle-cut on each end will result in vertical end faces. Facenail outer rafters to the crosspiece and tops of corner studs. The inner rafter facenails to the midpoints of the crosspiece and the top plate.

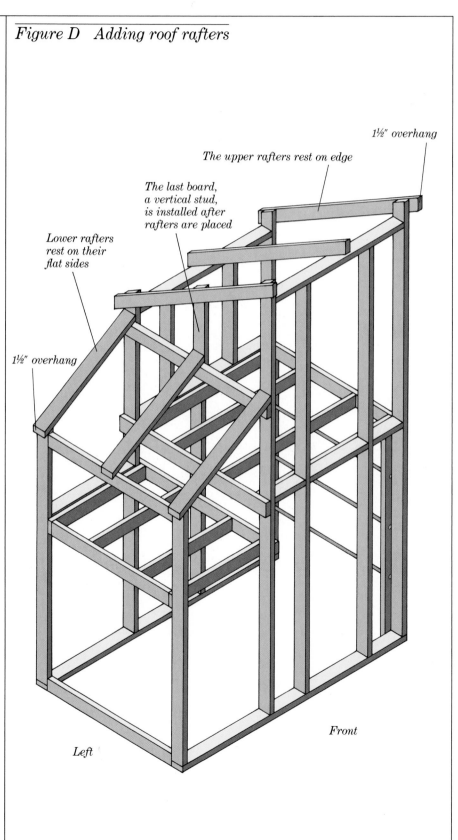

Figure D   Adding roof rafters

1½″ overhang

The upper rafters rest on edge

The last board, a vertical stud, is installed after rafters are placed

Lower rafters rest on their flat sides

1½″ overhang

Left

Front

The roof panels

Cut both roof panels from one sheet of 4 by 8 plywood (see Figure F-2). The photograph of the playhouse shows a roof made of ⅜-inch plywood siding. This roof is stained to match the sides but could be covered with strips of roll roofing nailed *at the rafters*. If you opt for a shingle roof,

use plywood roof sheathing that is thick enough to prevent roofing nails from protruding through bottom (¾-inch sheet minimum; 1⅛-inch is better). Cut plywood panels so that they are flush with edges and ends of rafters (Figure E), and nail them with 4d galvanized box nails. Use 6d or larger for thicker sheathing. Space nails every 5 inches.

One last piece

Fit a short vertical 2 by 4—the "last stud"—to the triangular vertical wall above the lower roof (Figure D). Facenail the bottom to the right side of the crosspiece and rafter end and the top to the right side of the upper rafter.

Figure E Attaching roof panels

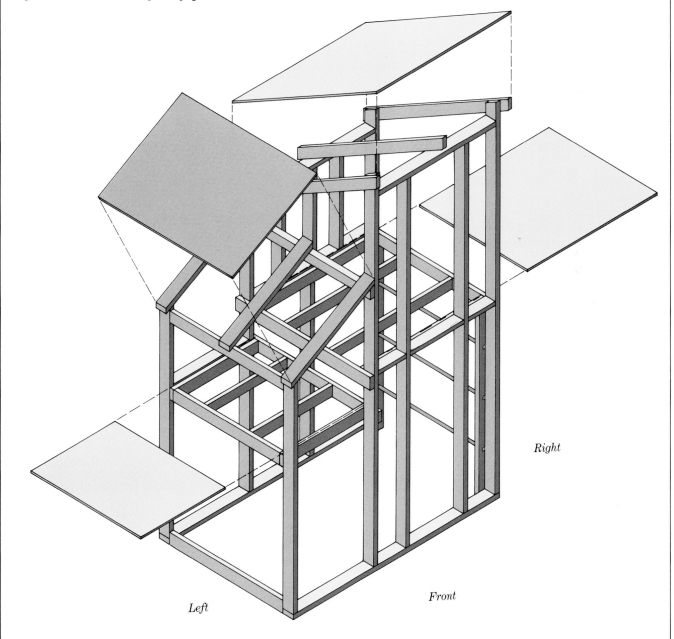

Right

Left

Front

Split-level Playhouse

Cover the walls

This playhouse uses ⅜-inch exterior-grade plywood siding. Figure F-2 shows how to cut wall panels from four sheets of 4 by 8 plywood. Follow the elevation drawings in Figure F-1 for layout and placement of panels. Use a nail, string, and pencil to mark the circular shapes. See the detail of this method shown on page 73. Cut openings with a saber saw or router before nailing panels in place. Observe the panel orientations in Figures F-1 and F-2. This will ensure that the grain runs vertically on all exterior panels.

It is best to take measurements directly from the playhouse frame and cut plywood accordingly. Just before nailing panels to frame, remove the temporary cross-braces from inside the playhouse. This allows you to square the walls to the plywood. The plywood is manufactured very square, so utilize as many original corners and edges as possible.

The plywood panel at the lower right of the back elevation is special. This panel attaches to a 2 by 2 nailing-frame, as shown in Figure F-3. Cut plywood to fit inside the window of the 2 by 4 framing. When in place, plywood should be flush with 2 by 4 framing.

Attach the ⅜-inch plywood walls with 4d galvanized box nails spaced every 6 inches. If you plan to use contrasting trim, stain or paint structure before installing trim.

Figure F-1 Placing wall panels

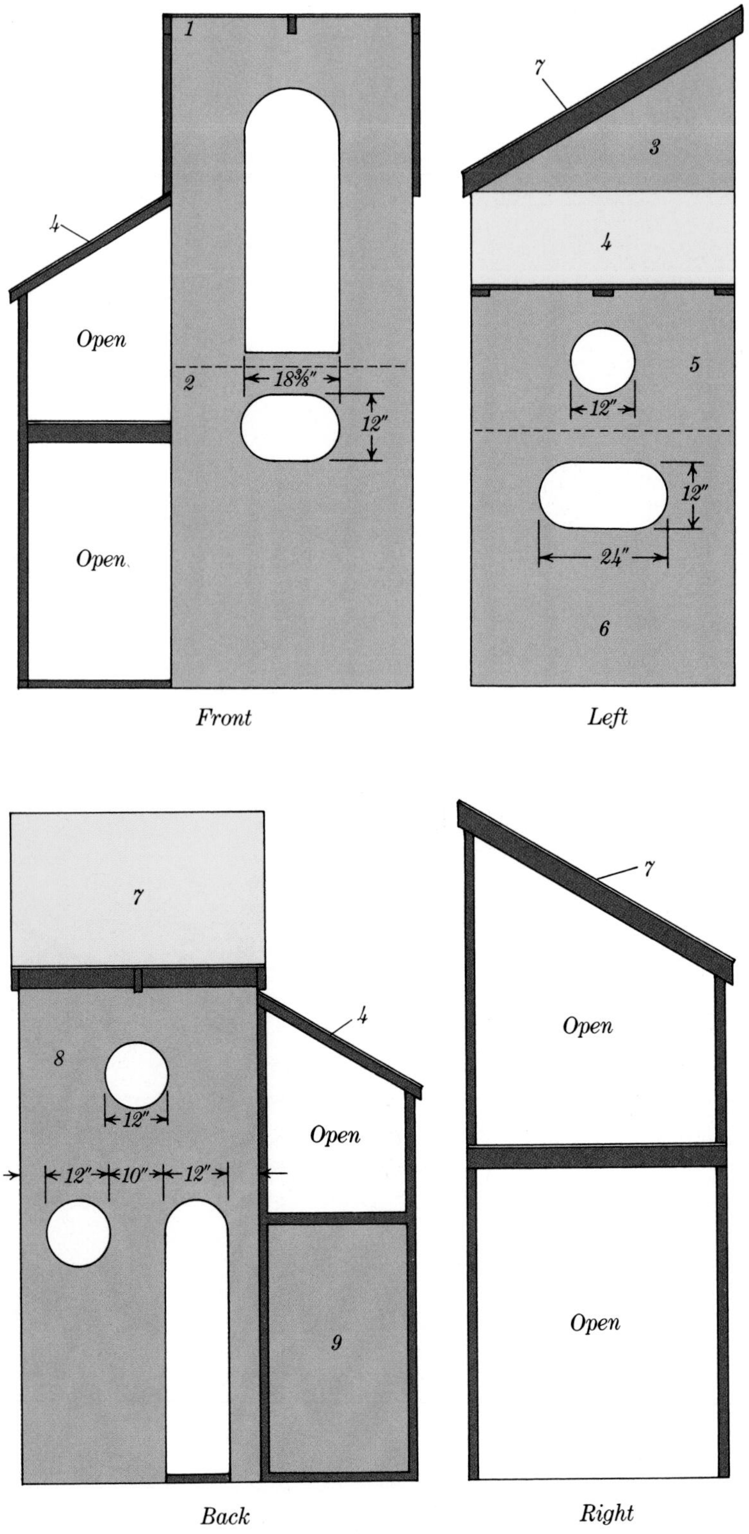

Front

Left

Back

Right

Figure F-2 Cutting wall panels

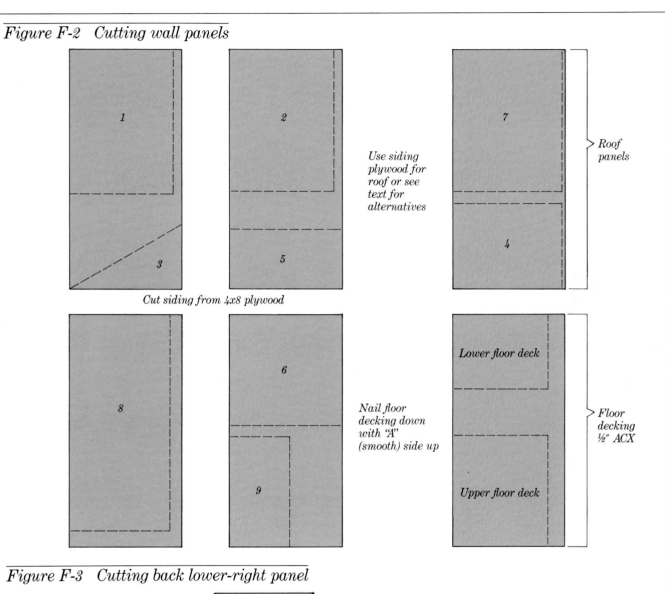

1

2

3

5

7

4

Use siding plywood for roof or see text for alternatives

Roof panels

Cut siding from 4x8 plywood

8

6

9

Nail floor decking down with "A" (smooth) side up

Lower floor deck

Upper floor deck

Floor decking ½" ACX

Figure F-3 Cutting back lower-right panel

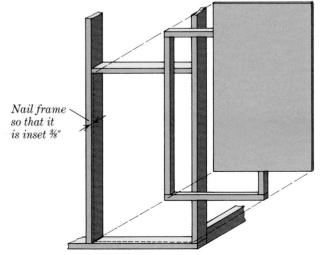

Nail frame so that it is inset ⅜"

Make nailing frame of 2x2s to fit into opening of lower back wall. Nail frame in place, inset ⅜" from the 2x4s. Then nail plywood to frame, flush with the 2x4s

Split-level Playhouse

Add the entry ladder

Make angle-cuts on the ends of two 2 by 4 rails, as shown in Figure G-1. Drill the rails with 1-inch holes for the pipe rungs, using the method detailed in Figure G-2. After securing rungs, attach ladder to structure by drilling ³/₁₆-inch holes and fitting four ¹/₄-inch by 3-inch lag screws with ¹/₄-inch washers under heads (Figure H).

Add horizontal ladder

The horizontal ladder attaches to the right side of the playhouse, as shown in Figure H. Use select structural fir for the 96-inch 2 by 6 rails, and redwood or pressure-treated 96-inch 4 by 4s for the posts.

Start by laying out rails. Locate holes for rungs centered 2¹/₂-inches down from top edge of rails.

Space the six rungs 14 inches on center along the rail, with 13-inch spaces at each end. Follow Figure G-2 for rung-to-rail attachment.

After assembling ladder, dig two footing holes 16 inches deep, centered 92³/₄-inches to the right of the playhouse corners. Complete instructions for making footings can be found on page 34. Place the 4 by 4s into the holes. Using four C-clamps, lift and clamp ladder to playhouse studs and posts. The tops of the rails should be 80 inches above the ground, but check and level the ladder as necessary.

Drill two ³/₁₆-inch holes 1¹/₄ inches from each edge of each rail at the end that will join the playhouse. Drive four ¹/₄-inch by 5-inch lag screws with flat washers to attach rails to playhouse studs. At the post end of each rail, drill two ³/₄-inch-diameter by ¹/₂-inch-deep counterbores and ¹/₄-inch throughbores through post and rail. Position these 1¹/₄ inches from rail edges. Secure rails to posts using ¹/₄-inch by 5-inch carriage bolts (with flat washers and nuts at the counterbore ends of bolts).

Add the add-ons

The Split-level Playhouse can be augmented with a variety of peripheral features. The swing beam described in the Creative Climber, page 76, can be attached above the horizontal ladder, running out behind the playhouse. Plans for the wave slide (shown in the photograph) appear on pages 26–27. A fire pole can be added; see page 74 for specifications. The bottom level can serve as a sandbox; see sandboxes on pages 32–33 for guidelines.

Select the swings

Select from a variety of swing units included on page 23, or order them from playground equipment suppliers listed on page 37.

Figure G-1   Entry ladder angle cuts

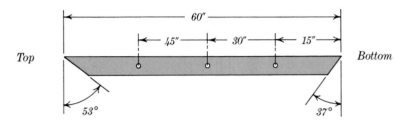

Top   60"   45"   30"   15"   Bottom

53°   37°

Figure G-2   Pipe rung attachment detail

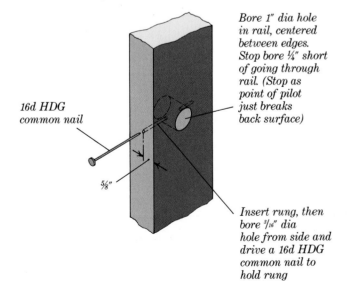

16d HDG common nail

⁵/₈"

Bore 1" dia hole in rail, centered between edges. Stop bore ¹/₄" short of going through rail. (Stop as point of pilot just breaks back surface)

Insert rung, then bore ³/₁₆" dia hole from side and drive a 16d HDG common nail to hold rung

Figure H   Adding entry and horizontal ladder

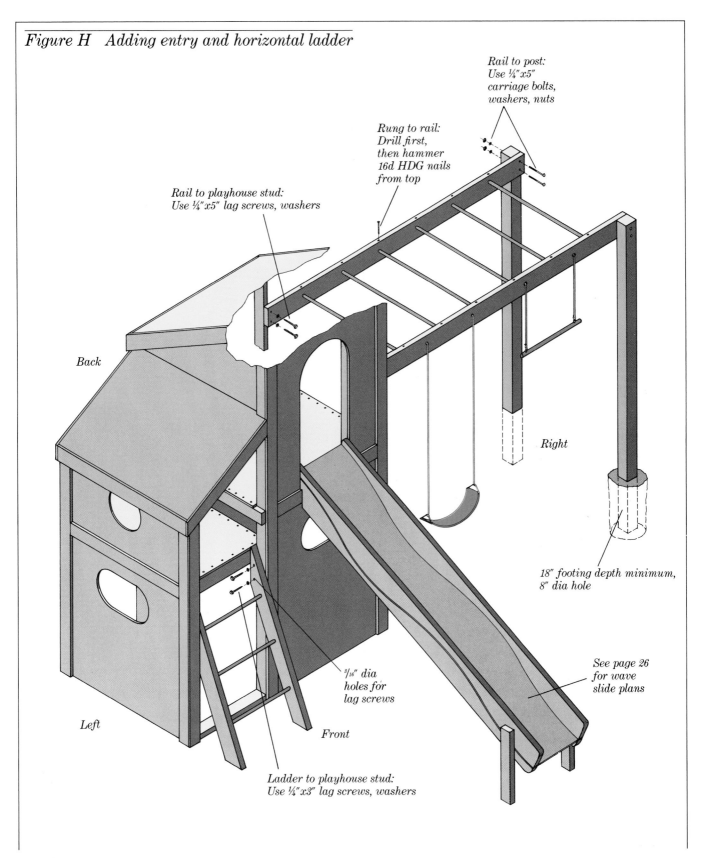

Rail to post:
Use ¼"x5"
carriage bolts,
washers, nuts

Rung to rail:
Drill first,
then hammer
16d HDG nails
from top

Rail to playhouse stud:
Use ¼"x5" lag screws, washers

Back

Right

18" footing depth minimum,
8" dia hole

Left

Front

³/₁₆" dia
holes for
lag screws

See page 26
for wave
slide plans

Ladder to playhouse stud:
Use ¼"x3" lag screws, washers

Split-level Playhouse

Attach the trim

If trim is to be stained or painted in a color that contrasts with the main structure, then cut all trim first, and stain or paint it before attaching.

Use 1 by 6 trim for the fascia boards around all roof edges (see Figure I). Angle-cut the ends of the raked pieces (mark them by holding them in position on the structure and scribing the cut line). Bevel-rip the top and bottom edges of the level fascia boards to match the roof angle (30 degrees from horizontal).

Make remaining trim from 1 by 4 stock. Nail into position as shown in Figure I, or create your own trim pattern. Nail all trim through plywood, into framing, to avoid exposed nails inside the structure. For 1-by trim, use 8d galvanized box nails.

Maintenance

The Split-level Playhouse, like the other projects, must be checked and tightened three months after completion. Repair or replace worn or damaged parts. Repeat the process six months and once a year thereafter.

Figure I   Attaching trim

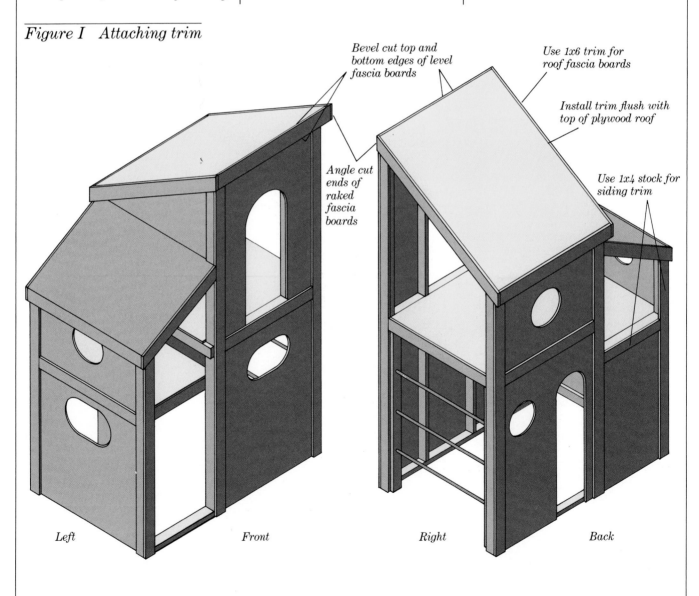

Bevel cut top and bottom edges of level fascia boards

Use 1x6 trim for roof fascia boards

Install trim flush with top of plywood roof

Angle cut ends of raked fascia boards

Use 1x4 stock for siding trim

Left   Front   Right   Back

The Split-level Playhouse, like the preceding projects, may be assembled in different sizes or in phases. The illustration shows the actual size of the structure with the slide, horizontal ladder, and swing. The approximate total area required is shown, as well as the play safety zone, as indicated by the loose loop around the project.

Split-level Playhouse with slide, horizontal ladder, and swing

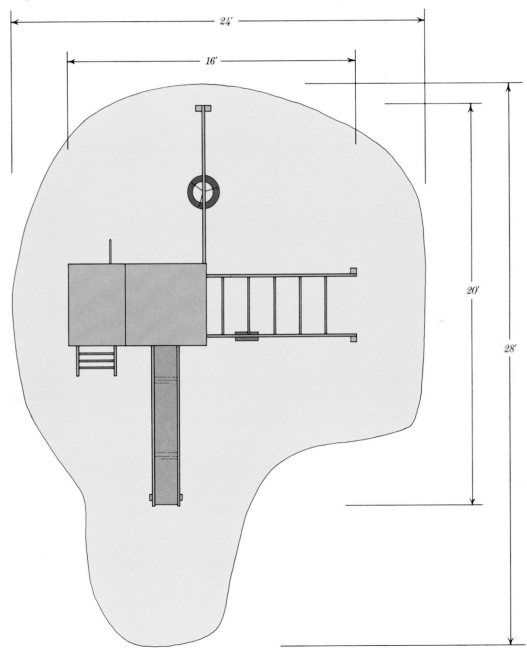

24′

16′

20′

28′

INDEX

U.S. Measure and Metric Measure Conversion Chart

		Formulas for Exact Measures			*Rounded Measures for Quick Reference*		
	Symbol	*When you know:*	*Multiply by:*	*To find:*			
Mass (Weight)	oz	ounces	28.35	grams	1 oz		= 30 g
	lb	pounds	0.45	kilograms	4 oz		= 115 g
	g	grams	0.035	ounces	8 oz		= 225 g
	kg	kilograms	2.2	pounds	16 oz	= 1 lb	= 450 kg
					32 oz	= 2 lb	= 900 kg
					36 oz	= 2¼ lb	= 1000g (a kg)
Volume	tsp	teaspoons	5.0	milliliters	¼ tsp	= 1/24 oz	= 1 ml
	tbsp	tablespoons	15.0	milliliters	½ tsp	= 1/12 oz	= 2 ml
	fl oz	fluid ounces	29.57	milliliters	1 tsp	= ⅙ oz	= 5 ml
	c	cups	0.24	liters	1 tbsp	= ½ oz	= 15 ml
	pt	pints	0.47	liters	1 c	= 8 oz	= 250 ml
	qt	quarts	0.95	liters	2 c (1 pt)	= 16 oz	= 500 ml
	gal	gallons	3.785	liters	4 c (1 qt)	= 32 oz	= 1 l
	ml	milliliters	0.034	fluid ounces	4 qt (1 gal)	= 128 oz	= 3¾- l
Length	in.	inches	2.54	centimeters	⅜ in.	= 1 cm	
	ft	feet	30.48	centimeters	1 in.	= 2.5 cm	
	yd	yards	0.9144	meters	2 in.	= 5 cm	
	mi	miles	1.609	kilometers	2½ in.	= 6.5 cm	
	km	kilometers	0.621	miles	12 in. (1 ft)	= 30 cm	
	m	meters	1.094	yards	1 yd	= 90 cm	
	cm	centimeters	0.39	inches	100 ft	= 30 m	
					1 mi	= 1.6 km	
Temperature	°F	Fahrenheit	5/9 (after subtracting 32)	Celsius	32°F	= 0°C	
					68°F	= 20°C	
	°C	Celsius	9/5 (then add 32)	Fahrenheit	212°F	= 100°C	
Area	in.^{2}	square inches	6.452	square centimeters	1 in.^{2}	= 6.5 cm^2	
	ft^2	square feet	929.0	square centimeters	1 ft^2	= 930 cm^2	
	yd^2	square yards	8361.0	square centimeters	1 yd^2	= 8360 cm^2	
	a	acres	0.4047	hectares	1 a	= 4050 m^2	